POTEMKIN, Inc.

HOW PERCEPTION IS EVERYTHING AND WHAT TO DO WITH IT IN BUSINESS

By

Philippe Joly

"This fun, controversial and original book teaches you how to dress up your small business for your clients the way you might impress a first date. The model Philippe suggests is the aftershave or perfume of the small business world. Perception mightn't be everything... but it's really, really important."

Owen Fitzpatrick
Entrepreneur, Best Selling Author

***

"A fascinating and touching guided-tour backstage into the reality of many small businesses run on a shoe string. A great gift for anyone thinking about starting a business, and a wonderful read even for more experienced entrepreneurs."

Paolo Rizzardini
Technology Entrepreneur

***

"One might wonder what 18th century Russian Empire could have to do with 21st century entrepreneurship and Start-Ups. A whole lot if it is Philippe Joly's profound and heartfelt personal tale that uses the legend of the Potemkin villages as an original look at modern entrepreneurship."

Guillaume Neu-Pietri
Professional Sailor, Sea and Sky Diver, and Entrepreneur

First Edition

ISBN: 978-1-4478-9530-5

Published by Philippe Joly

Credits:

Inside illustration by Giuseppe Detto "Pino" Onorati

***

Contact the author:

Philippe Joly

info@potemkininc.com

***

Visit the Potemkin, Inc. website for more information:

www.potemkininc.com

CONTENTS

This book is dedicated to hardworking entrepreneurs, men and women, who make sacrifices every day in order to take action on their dreams, despite other people telling them how crazy they are, that it cannot be done, that they are too old or too young, or that they should simply get a safe job like anyone else.

For my mother, friends and family, who always supported me in my entrepreneurial journey and still continue to do so today.

A special thought goes to my dear wife and our lovely little girls.

ABOUT THE AUTHOR

Philippe Joly is a French entrepreneur born in Russia in 1976.

He grew up in France, where he arrived as a baby, but it is in Ireland that his entrepreneurial journey started in 2005, when he left his stable managerial job to start his first business.

He is polyglot in many European languages and a well-travelled entrepreneur, whose expertise and passion for mobile and web technologies get him regularly solicited for consultancy work all over the world.

Philippe has been involved in many projects in the digital space including mobile apps, web portals, social networks, location-based services, social media, backup services, online video, mobile web and mobile security.

He was nominated for various entrepreneurial awards and won the Mobile Messaging Award in 2011 with his latest venture, SafeBox, which attracted over one million users in just a year and is sold worldwide by the largest mobile operators and content providers.

Philippe has lived and worked in France, the former Soviet Union, Ireland, Italy and Hong Kong.

PREFACE

Have you ever noticed that when people hear of someone, who owns a business, many tend to focus immediately on the monetary aspect?

People do not seem to know that you can open a business for less money than you would spend on a good night out in a nightclub.

Many do not realise that having your own business also offers far more valuable things than money, and that for a long time, it may even offer those valuable things, instead of money.

They seem to miss the unprecedented sense of freedom and control over your life that you get from running your own business.

How to transmit to someone external to this environment the freedom of being able to do what you want, go where you want, and create whatever product goes through your mind?

How to make them really appreciate the satisfaction of seeing a product, which came out of your idea, for sale on the shelves of a shop? Whether it sells or not is secondary to the satisfied feeling that someone out there is using your product to resolve his problem, or that what you do adds value to others.

If I think about the people, the friends, the enemies, the travels, the fame, and the fun, there is no doubt for me that an entrepreneurial journey is worthwhile, even independently of the financial reward it may or may not bring.

It would be a lie to say that money is not important. It does play a serious role and is an integral part of the development phases, which can turn your idea into a viable business and it is also a very enjoyable reward for your efforts.

But while thinking about this book and looking back at my own experience and that of friends and other entrepreneurs, I came to realise that one other aspect has far more importance than anything else, even more than money.

I did not see it described in any books or manuals, and it was certainly not taught in business school, but after a few months of knocking at the doors of investors with my first business plan in hands, I discovered that there was a new 80/20 rule to apply:

The twenty you show and the eighty you don't.

I realised that their perception of me, and the credibility that I conveyed, were the key factors that could make or break my entrepreneurial dream, and most importantly that their perception could be manipulated to see one thing or another.

I have called it the "Potemkin" phase, inspired by the Potemkin villages legend, which I have once been told on a business trip to Russia, and which I will describe in more details in this book.

In an economic crisis, like the one we live in right now, the spirit of entrepreneurship gets stimulated.

Logically, people start thinking that if they cannot find a job, they could create their own.

Start-Ups flourish and the word *Start-Up* has now become a real *buzz word* across borders and cultures.

The market is getting flooded with websites, books, products and services designed to help young Start-Ups promote their business.

However, most of what I have tested, did add little real credibility to my business and some tools were even counter-productive.

Let's be serious, having *10 votes*, *16 Tweets*, *25 Facebook Likes* and 200 fans does not give any real credibility to a business, does it?

In this book, I have tried to describe a kind of credibility that can convince someone to invest over half a million Euros into a one-man band, help close international deals, make you respected by your peers and recognised in your industry, attract a significant and large customer base, and get leading media interested in your business.

There are many "How-to" books written about success, achievement, starting a business, entrepreneurship and so on, but I would like to think that this book is *not* one of them, and offers something different and more personal.

I wrote this book in the spirit of short story-telling based on my own personal experience that I wanted to share with other young entrepreneurs.

I did not want to write another book on theories, techniques, attitudes, and secrets to become a successful entrepreneur.

Those types of books count in thousands and can be found anywhere.

Most of them sell courses or other books by the same writer, often talk about people, who succeeded in business fifty years ago, abuse of famous quotes in every chapter, and ultimately look and feel like they have been published by a marketing machine of manufacturing money-making books rather than genuine books telling a real story that you can truly relate to.

I am sure that you know what kind of books I am referring to.

Over the past ten years, I have read a lot of them, I went to many courses, I got certificates giving me qualifications in this and that, I bought the CD's, did the exercises, and even met some of the world's most acclaimed "gurus".

But as a young European entrepreneur living in the Age of Internet, mobile phones, viral marketing, and social media, I found it hard to really relate to W. Clement Stone, Carnegie, or Napoleon Hill or many other authors, who lead the business and personal achievement book charts.

I did get a lot of knowledge and motivation from reading them, going to courses and meeting even briefly some of the most respected experts in the field of personal achievement and business.

I am thinking much faster and better as a result, and I even try to always live my life with passion like Tony Robbins taught me to.

But a lot of books I have read about entrepreneurship and success were written by people, who either had not done what they preached but rather described what other people had done, or were written by people, who had achieved something extraordinary such a long time ago that they could not remember anymore how they felt back then, and did not do anything else since, except writing books as a business of talking about their past achievements.

This is only my humble opinion, so do not get offended if you happened to have read or even written the handful of books that are excluded from this description.

I wanted to find a book describing something original, something new, something personal that I could really relate to, something that could inspire me and help grow my business; a book that was written by someone, who was currently experiencing the same as I was experiencing, felt the same solitude, had similar anecdotes, and was at the same stage of the entrepreneurial journey as I was.

I could not find one, so I decided to write my own.

Despite the appearances, you will notice that this book is not about entrepreneurial success, but about the entrepreneurial journey, which I personally found far more challenging and interesting.

My goal in writing this book is to pin-point a concept that I have discovered over the years and found far more fundamental than any of the other rules they teach in business school.

If after reading this book you understand the concept of the Potemkin villages and how it relates to modern Start-Ups, and if it helps you make your entrepreneurial journey less chaotic, more enjoyable and make the rewards come faster, then I would have achieved my goal.

Whether you will be successful or not, depends entirely upon you.

Examples of people, who started from nothing and succeeded, are many, but examples of people, who had everything to succeed, and did not, are far more.

While I have learnt that there are *many* reasons not to start in business and not to leave your existing stability, I have also learnt that there are *many more* reasons to start a business and enter into this rollercoaster of emotions, uncertainties, surprises and rewards that Start-Up life has to offer.

Not all entrepreneurs really want to become the new Steve Jobs, Bill Gates, Warren Buffett, Larry Page, Sergey Brin or Mark Zuckerberg, by the way.

Most entrepreneurs I know simply want to turn their ideas into a successful business and enjoy everything that the entrepreneurial world has to offer.

They know fully well that they will not change the world with their ventures, and that is OK, as long as they change *their* world.

There is a quote that summarises well in my opinion the reason why I chose to become an entrepreneur and what I have been trying to get out of it, ever since.

I would gladly give the credit for this quote to its legitimate owner, but I saw it used by so many different people that it is unclear to me, who said it first. I will give the credit to Anthony Robbins, as I first read it in one of his books and he is one, who in my opinion, walks his talk very well.

The quote says that being truly successful means *doing "what we want", "when we want", "where we want", "with whom we want" and "as much as we want".*

This is the vision that has been fuelling my entrepreneurial journey from the very beginning and that continues to do so today.

Along the way to this ultimate goal, I have discovered Potemkin and his villages and this significantly accelerated the process for me.

INTRODUCTION

This book is my adaptation of the Potemkin villages to modern entrepreneurship, using some true stories and anecdotes that I have experienced during my own entrepreneurial journey.

Some of you may already be familiar with the term *Potemkin villages*, but to better put this book into context, this introduction is a good place for some historical background about the *original* Potemkin villages legend.

Let's familiarise ourselves with Potemkin and his villages and go back a few hundred years ago, to 18th century Russia.

Back then, the Russian Empire was ruled by Catherine The Great, who took over after the death of her husband.

During her long reign, she managed to transform, revitalise, expand, and modernise Russia to become one of the greatest powers of Europe.

One man in her Court contributed a lot to this success.

His name was Prince Grigori Alexandrovich Potyomkin, better known as *Potemkin*.

He had been the Empress' lover for a while and for that intimate relationship, was referred to as her *favourite*.

And favouritism there was indeed, as he was appointed to a series of very important posts, from Minister to Commander-in-Chief of the Russian army, among the other many titles he was given, including the title of Prince, which he received as a gift.

In 1783, under the leadership of Potemkin, Russia continued its campaign of expansion and conquered the under-developed region of Crimea (in modern-day Ukraine).

Potemkin added another title to his already long list and became Governor General of the Crimea region.

This region was in a very strategic location on the Black Sea, and Potemkin had great plans to exploit it.

He wanted to build an impressive arsenal and create an immense war fleet.

He also wanted to transform this desolated land into one of the most prosperous parts of the Russian Empire by building new towns and splendid palaces, creating new enterprises, and attracting settlers from other parts of Russia in order to colonise this region and develop it.

The story of the Potemkin villages began a few years later, when under pressure from foreign ambassadors represented at her Court the Empress had to demonstrate to everyone that her Empire was indeed the great Russia they had heard of.

Potemkin's great conquest of the Crimea was the perfect showcase of the prosperity she wanted to demonstrate.

She told Potemkin that she wanted to visit her newly acquired land and show off Russia's prosperity to foreign powers. Naturally, she put Potemkin in charge of organising everything.

What the Empress did not know, was that the region was still a vast construction field and apart from the odd villages and a few roads here and there, there were no palaces or any real prosperity to show for, yet.

Potemkin had focused his energy primarily on the military aspects in order to take advantage of the strategic region.

While the construction of his gigantic arsenal was indeed in a good way, other less strategic parts of his original plan had not progressed.

To make things worse, Crimea was becoming a region in turmoil, a desolated land, where frustrated peasants were living in poverty, and where mutinies were becoming common occurrence.

With Catherine The Great and her foreign guests on their way, Potemkin had to find a way to give the perception to everyone that this vast region was peaceful and prosperous in order to impress the Royal cortege with the high value of his work.

He did not know where to start, but being put in charge of organising everything was already a good starting point.

One day, as he was sitting outside, looking at the river and relying on the national beverage for inspiration, an ambitious plan started to emerge.

Potemkin approached the Empress and suggested a boat trip along the Dnieper River.

The Dnieper runs across the whole country, all the way to the Black sea.

He presented the boat trip as a great solution to give Her Majesty and her guests the best insight into his entire conquest, in just one trip.

The boat trip was indeed a very clever move, as Potemkin had intentionally restricted the entire trip to a limited and controllable area, a river.

The legend goes that Potemkin built fake villages along the desolated banks of the river, where he had confined the route of the Royal visit.

He constructed painted wooden facades of splendid houses that he erected in front of crumbling and basic structures.

Peasants were dressed up in beautiful clothes in advance of the Empress' arrival.

They were fed and ordered to dance and chant.

Some cattle and animals were also brought in to add to the prosperity he needed to portray.

Each night, the wooden facades, the animals and the people were transported to the next stop along the route for the next planned *performance*.

There is no need to explain how ambitious and risky this plan was.

But Potemkin had no choice. The risk of not making this visit a success was far greater.

Firstly, he was in need of more funding to complete his work, so he had to remain in the good favours of the Empress.

But most importantly, the single idea of making the Empress lose face in front of the foreign powers that were putting her under pressure, would have most certainly been fatal for him, literally, favourite or not.

The *Potemkin villages*, as they came to be known later, did work.

Potemkin managed to fool the Empress, who happily returned to her palace and never asked to visit her land again.

She gave him more funding to continue his beautiful work and relied fully on Potemkin from then onwards.

His ruse had also impressed the foreign ambassadors present on this trip.

The Potemkin villages contributed to increase the perception that the Russian Empire was one of the most prosperous and powerful in Europe.

This perception then created further partnership opportunities, which in turn, reinforced Russia's real power and prosperity.

Over the centuries, the Potemkin villages concept has been used and reused countless times and is now commonly known as a false construct, either physical or figurative, built to hide an undesirable or potentially damaging reality.

Mostly visible in political contexts, the Potemkin villages are about presenting something great as if it was the rule, not the exception.

China has always been a big fan of the Potemkin villages. As a recent example, during the 2008 Beijing Olympics, foreign journalists referred to Potemkin Olympic villages.

In the former Soviet Union, back in Communist times and the Cold War, Potemkin's approach was also frequently used to fool foreign visitors by showing selected villages, factories, schools, stores, or neighbourhoods and present them as if they were typical.

The Potemkin villages are used to give a perception that everything is good by showing a small selected sample and making it seem as the normality rather than the exception.

The fact that access to anything else that what you are showing is not given, is one of the key elements of the Potemkin concept.

Wherever movement of visitors is strictly limited, the Potemkin villages are very efficient, as it is impossible for visitors to see any other example.

This approach has also been used in business for a very long time, but unlike in politics, it can serve a far more positive goal, especially for small businesses.

For the *Potemkin, Inc. Start-Ups* that I will describe in this book, it should not be seen as a ruse to fool people.

A thief is someone, who steals from someone else and a con artist is a confidence trickster, who makes someone else give him money of his own will, in exchange for thin air.

The Potemkin entrepreneurs are *neither* of them.

They are committed entrepreneurs, who are serious about their business, have products or services with great potential, but just need to create opportunities to push them out of the initial bootstrapped phase and put their business on its feet.

While they can use the Potemkin approach to create a favourable perception and hide a potentially damaging reality in order to seize an opportunity, they later *must* deliver on their promises and walk their talk, risking more bad than good otherwise.

If they do not deliver, they create the opposite effect and simply become one of the above two types.

First-time entrepreneurs are normal people, like you and me, who one day have a terrific idea that they believe so good to convince themselves to leave their stable job, invest all their savings, or even borrow money, and start their own business.

They are risk-takers, who take action to go after their dream, whatever their dream may be, money, fame, success, or simply self-satisfaction of having turned an idea into something concrete.

From day one, the clock starts ticking, and their success depends on their ability to rapidly create a viable business out of their idea.

This means creating an attractive product, promoting it efficiently, finding customers, closing deals and generating sufficient revenues to exceed the costs, and all of this in an often crowded market.

Many manage to do it, but many others naturally struggle.

How do you turn an idea into a successful business, when you have never done it before, have little or no money, do not even know where to start, nobody knows that you exist, and of course you have no customers yet?

In this book, I will take you through my own entrepreneurial journey with stories and anecdotes that show various types of Potemkin villages in action.

Some are concrete physical villages, while others are more abstract and relate to a specific mind-set.

The Start-Up journey is made of ups and downs, but while the ups are the most enjoyable parts, it is the downs that are probably the most valuable in the long term.

For this reason, I have focused some stories and anecdotes on the lower moments, in order to illustrate how difficult entrepreneurial life may become at times, and show that any hurdles, mistakes, or disappointments can be overcome by understanding that running a Start-Up is like a game, in which building Potemkin villages and having fun can make a real difference.

I have tried to create a cosy atmosphere for this book, like a friend telling a story to another. I even occasionally left some F words for the purpose of better identifying with my thoughts or feelings in certain circumstances, as I would have in a spoken conversation.

By letting the readers know me better and by sharing my personal stories and anecdotes, I hope to have achieved the reading experience, which I had in mind, and that you will enjoy my adaptation of the Potemkin villages to modern entrepreneurship.

I wish every reader success with their Potemkin, Inc. ventures.

"Potemkin, Inc. - A New Generation Of Potemkin Villages"

JUST KEEP SWIMMING

Everyone knows that running a business takes time and persistence, and that overnight success stories are rare. But what many may not realise, is that some of the hard times of Start-Up life do also impact, besides the obvious finances, your social interactions, your families and your relationships.

There are times, when you come to question yourself on whether to continue or stop, because you cannot take it anymore.

The only thing that keeps you going is the firm belief in what you are doing.

You keep focused and you keep going, no matter what, like an athlete going for Gold. You fall, dust yourself off, get back on your feet and continue.

Let me tell you a story about one of those low moments.

It's 9:15am, and there is already a small queue at the bank. My turn arrives and I patiently wait for the clerk to finish reordering his desk and give me some attention. We greet each other and I hand him over some foreign banknotes that I want to change into Euros.

He checks the notes, checks the exchange rate on his computer, pauses, looks at me, then looks at his computer once more, looks at me again and says:

"Do you know that there is a commission on each of these transactions?"

I knew. I was about to change less than fifteen Euros in four different currencies, which after the bank's commission would give me just a few coins.

He asked me if I was sure, I nodded positively, filled the forms and completed the transaction.

I was calm and had a smile on my face, as I took the coins that he was handing me over the counter, with an air of confusion.

Why was he so confused? you may ask.

He was not so much confused about the low amount, although it may have seemed a bit ridiculous to change such a small amount of money and pay the bank more commission than what I received. The real reason behind his confusion was the fact that I was wearing a suit and tie, had a nice leather briefcase, wore a quality watch, and looked like a wealthy businessman, and this, contrasted completely with the transaction that had just happened.

What the clerk didn't know was that those coins he just gave me were the only things I had left and saved my day.

That day, I was not poor with less than a few hundred in my bank account; I had nothing at all in my bank account.

In fact, I did not have any money left at all, not in the bank, not in my wallet, not under my mattress, no money left anywhere, not enough money to buy food even. The night before, I had some boiled water with oil, salt and pepper as a soup for dinner. That's how bad it was.

I am not trying to paint a picture of the poor guy, who touched the bottom and climbed his way back up. I have been fortunate, even at the worse times, to always have a roof over my head and not experience what a lot of people living in the streets unfortunately do every day. But *that* day, I had less than the street beggar in his paper cup.

In terms of pure financial situation, I was as broke as you could be. Not a penny left…Nothing, zilch, nada!

I had sold everything that I owned, from guitars to electronics, books, and anything that had any monetary value and could be sold quickly and easily.

I had borrowed money from my family, my friends and everyone I knew, even from people, whom I barely knew.

I had taken everything I could from anyone, and whichever way I was looking at it, I was broke, and I was hungry, literally, not just for success.

I had to find a solution to fix *today*'s short-term crisis.

I was not really worried about tomorrow, as today was my absolute priority. Tomorrow would be another story possibly, like some yesterdays had been.

In those situations, you enter into a profound thinking process, where you review, one by one, like a slide show, everything and everyone you know, going back all the way to high-school, in order to find a way to get some money, any money at all.

And then it struck me.

"I must have some foreign bank notes somewhere, left from previous travelling", I thought.

These bank notes were certainly not as useful, where they currently were, picking up dust, as they would be in my pocket, changed into valid currency.

The point of this story is that an injection of cash, no matter how little, can save you for one day and give you a boost of strength to continue thinking about running your business instead of more basic needs for survival.

Later that morning, after the most enjoyable cup of coffee I have ever had and a well-needed breakfast, I began thinking about how to get out of the trouble I was currently in.

I sat in my small office, which of course I had not yet paid rent for, and I started thinking about how to get immediate cash. Legally of course, although I must admit that other ways had crossed my mind too, as the situation was becoming desperate.

I called the bank to try to get another overdraft, they refused.

I called creditors, asking them to pay immediately what they owed my company, only to hear back annoyingly that the cheque was already in the post, as I had already heard many weeks before.

These lies pissed me off, but none of this was resolving my problem of *today*.

I was running out of time and energy to waste in battling against secretaries, zealously protecting their employer from people like me, asking them for money that they actually did owe me, but were only prepared to pay on their fantasist terms rather than our signed contractual agreement.

It became clear to me that in the next six hours, I had to find a way create an opportunity out of nowhere, make a winning sales pitch, sign a deal and get paid for it.

What could I do?

Thinking at length about what I was skilled at, and what I could sell to get cash fast enough, I finally found an angle.

I was going to find someone, who needed a website. After all, I had been building websites for years and was rather good at it.

But I was in a hurry, so I needed to look locally, and out of the one million people living in Dublin, there had to be *one* person, who needed a website badly.

A website would not cost me any money at all, just some time, some creativity and some hard work. But in the end, I could produce, out of nothing, something that has a monetary value.

Skilled web developers were still an expensive treat for Start-Ups, so building a website was the perfect way out of my financial crisis.

All I needed now was a customer.

I made a list of people to target.

Then, making good use of my still miraculously working phone line, I started to call them one by one, asking if they or anyone they knew would need a website built as soon as possible, at a very competitive price.

Fortunately, early in the list, someone had a friend of a friend, who was looking for someone to help him create a website for his new business venture.

That was my opportunity to get out of this short-term financial struggle.

Our phone conversation was brief, but fruitful.

In fact, the guy recognised my name. There were not too many French people in my line of business in Ireland back then. He remembered having read an article about me in a business magazine. This obviously made for a friendly conversation and made my sales pitch easier.

He asked to meet me that same evening, and in good Irish tradition, suggested that we met in a pub to discuss the project after work.

"In the fecken pub!" I thought, discouraged.

A pub meant buying a round of drinks and therefore meant finding not less than 30 Euros to handle that meeting.

I barely managed to get a few coins that morning. How was I going to create more out of nothing for that evening?

I was running out of time, but there was no doubt that I had to seize this opportunity, which would give me some much needed breathing space for the rest of the month and allow me to pay rent, buy food and keep focusing on my business.

Preparing myself very well for that meeting was critical in order to be able to drive the conversation quickly around "which version do you prefer?" rather than "are you going to use me to build your website?"

I started by investing a few hours in researching his industry to have a feel for what his company's website could look like, what the company would do, and who else was already doing it.

Then, I prepared an analysis on his competitors' websites, designed a few mock-ups with various variations and wrote detailed explanations for each aspect of my designs.

There was a bit of fluff of course, but I felt that it was needed to produce a sizeable and more credible proposition document.

What happened next was a mix of creativity and improvisation with the faith that everything was going to be ok.

I arrived at the pub in advance and waited outside for the guy to arrive.

I still didn't have a penny. I had used every minute available to prepare for that meeting.

When he arrived, we shook hands and as he was about to move towards the entrance of the pub, I interrupted him and said, that I needed to take some cash first.

We went around the corner to the ATM and I put my card in, knowing fully well that I would not hear the enjoyable flapping noise of the notes being counted, and that no money could possibly come out.

Calmly, I entered the wrong PIN three times so that the ATM would swallow my card.

I then started agitating myself and went on about the fact that all of a sudden the machine gave a strange system error and did not give my card back, adding a bit of panicked look, talking about how late it was and that the bank was closed and so on.

I made a drama. Not too big, just focused on the fact that I was left with no money until tomorrow because of *this* misadventure and the stupid ATM machine.

Remember that I was not playing the part of an artistic web designer dude out of college.

I was wearing a suit and tie and was a credible internet expert, whom he had already heard of and read about in a respected magazine, and who was referred to him by a friend.

The guy would have never thought for a second that I had done this on purpose because I had nothing but a few useless coins in my pocket.

Ironically, he probably even had the perception that a guy like me would be too expensive for him.

How could he imagine that at that precise moment I could build his website in exchange for a sandwich?

I composed myself, closed my wallet, and said to the guy that we should get started with our meeting anyway, as I wanted to show him the mock-ups that I had already prepared for him. I would sort this situation out, somehow, after we had finished our working session.

He was very surprised that I had already prepared something for him so quickly, and was of course very interested in having a look.

We entered the pub and discussed his venture and website for an hour. During this short time, I had to ensure that I gave all the knowledge that I had so that he was quickly impressed, while making sure that he would not get scared, thinking that I would cost him a lot.

In fact, I used our common's friend relationship and my understanding of *his* Start-Up situation to justify a very low pricing.

I know what you think. It was sneaky. And you are right.

But this cunning approach kept the focus on him and made him think that I was doing him a favour. I had put him in a comfort zone to close the sale.

Closing a sale is a lot about *you, you, you*, rather than *me, me, me*.

He liked the designs very much, and we basically closed the deal there and then, discussed the timings, agreed the commercial terms and shook hands.

He seemed happier than me to have closed that deal. Apparently he had been looking for some help on this project for a while, and kept getting outrageous quotations.

We agreed to meet again later that week and go through the paperwork and other details.

I still had no money at all and surviving another few days would be very challenging.

However, I could reasonably expect some money in the next few days coming from the advance payment on that website, so I was a little relieved, but still broke as a joke.

Feeling that we were both at ease with each other and had moved from the business conversation to some casual chit-chat, I told him, looking annoyed:

"I have to go. I still have to sort out the stupid thing of the ATM machine."

I looked at my watch, frowned, paused, looked at him and with a smile, I added:

"I'll tell you what! I will give you a further discount on the price we just agreed if I can borrow 50 Euros from you to sort me out for tonight, so I can get home and so on without all this hassle. I'll give it back to you when we meet again on Thursday."

He laughed, and said, "Sounds good. Don't worry about it. Let's have another pint and you'll go home after."

God bless the Irish spirit!

Big laughs followed, his laugh was genuine I think, mine was a nervous laugh of relief.

Eventually, we stayed for another two hours, bonded well, had dinner in the pub that he paid for, and he gave me 50 Euros when we left the pub. So I had a free dinner, free drinks, and 50 Euros.

I did owe this money to a person that I had only met a few hours before, but I also got myself a deal that would resolve my immediate financial situation for a few weeks and I could focus on my business rather than food and rent.

I paid him back the next time we met, out of his own money, and all went smoothly.

My way out of this situation was completely improvised and driven by desperation but the important part of what happened was that I was conveying enough credibility to render *unthinkable* the thought that anything else was going on, other than what he perceived as the reality.

The credibility of what I looked like, what he had heard and read, what I had shown him, and the referral of a common friend made all this work.

The Potemkin approach is not always about a physical construction, it is often, like in this case, a more figurative façade, a mind-set with a matching appearance and behaviour.

By taking control of the conversation and the events, I controlled the perception and only gave access to the information that I wanted to give access to, like Potemkin did by controlling the river.

GAME ON

As I left the corporate world to start my first business, many people surrounding me, ex-colleagues, friends and family, could not understand at all what I was doing, and why I was doing it.

They were seeing me working countless hours, and struggling financially, with no apparent results.

In their mind, I had left behind a stable managerial position in a multi-national in order to start something on my own, from scratch, out of just an idea, and without any guaranty of success or safety nets to fall back into.

Their surprise and confusion were natural.

In fact, my friends and family were conditioned by the "corporate world" and some belonged to an older generation, whose reference points about starting a business were totally out-of-date, so the reality of modern Start-Ups was a mystery to them.

I bet that my mother still does not really understand what I am doing for a living, even after all these years.

Most entrepreneurs rapidly enter into a way of thinking that is hard to communicate and completely unknown to others, foreign to the Start-Up environment.

The corporate world and the Start-Up world can be seen as two games, which like any other games have rules, stages, good times and bad times, winners and losers.

The two games are *very* different, and while one offers a relative stability, the other is the complete opposite.

The "corporate game" has simple and defined rules.

Bluntly put, you have a job title with an associated job description and a monthly pay check.

You get paid for doing your job and if you do it well, you get promoted to a better job title with a better pay check.

Most decisions are made upstairs for you to simply follow.

The corporate game is like a race to get the best job title and best pay check possible.

However, there is a catch in the corporate game, and people know and fully accept it.

For the entire duration of the corporate game, you will always navigate in a defined range of income and your highest income will never, or rarely, exceed the maximum income available in your scale, based on your job description, experience, and skills.

In contrast, the rules of the "Start-Up game" are far more complex and less defined.

From the first day, you make your own job title. You can become CEO, president, managing director, chairman or any other fancy job title you want to give yourself, and therefore it often means very little.

You have no guaranty of a pay check at the end of the month, which can mean real personal financial struggle.

You make your own decisions, good and bad, and your job description changes every day to include many different jobs such as project manager, product manager, marketing manager, accountant, lawyer, salesman, web designer, software developer, cleaner, electrician, system administrator, courier, receptionist, and so on.

External factors that you have no control over, can rewrite the rules at any time, and send you back to the drawing board, when you least expect it.

These are two very different games that require two very different mind-sets.

Furthermore, one game has limited income levels, while the other, has unlimited but "potential" income.

I can think of many people, who have sold their businesses for seven or eight-digit figures and some people have even become billionaires out their business ventures.

While in the corporate world, a highly successful person navigates within six-digits and extremely rarely exceeds it.

The truth is that I cannot think of any other ways that can make you earn as much money as running your own business.

You could win the lotto or inherit a forgotten uncle's fortune, but let's face it none of it is likely to happen. And even if it did happen, I doubt that the satisfaction would be the same, but that would be another debate.

There is no doubt that money is one of the motivations for starting your own business, but I am convinced that it is a mistake to see money as the *only* motivation.

In fact, financial rewards are only *potential*, and your own business may earn you less money than you were earning in your stable corporate job. For a long time, it did for me and many other entrepreneurs I know.

Cheap, fast and easy does not exist and if the financial rewards come, they often do after an expensive, long and hard journey.

I believe that the *real* values of entrepreneurship are elsewhere.

They start from the absolute freedom you have, the complete control over your own life, the feeling that what you do adds value to others, the satisfaction of seeing your idea on the shelves of a shop, seeing people that you don't know use your product either to resolve a problem or to entertain themselves, the people you meet, the friends you make, the exotic travels, and the list could go on and on and on.

These are just few of the hundreds of reasons, other than money, that make the entrepreneurial journey worthwhile.

The money, if any, arrives towards the end of the journey.

I believe that it is a mistake to focus too much on the monetary aspect of entrepreneurship from the start because it will look after itself if you focus on each step of the journey and play the game right.

I have started my first business just to do something about what I thought was a good idea and try to turn it into something concrete.

Then, I saw that it could make money. But little did I know that it would not matter as much as the personal and professional experience that I would receive along the way.

How could I know that one idea would lead to another, that I would be starting many more ventures, having many more ideas, that I would be nominated for awards, win awards, be in the newspapers, give interviews, meet some of the most respected business people, relocate to live in three different countries, pitch for seven digits funding rounds, travel the world, be involved in projects for world-leading companies, become fluent in new languages, meet with millionaires and billionaires, and master new skills that command a level of income twice higher than most of my friends', and enjoy living on an island, thousands of miles away from where I grew up?

How could I know?

They don't tell you all that in business school or in books about starting a business.

The truth is that if I had focused only on money from the start, I would have stopped just six month later, when I ran out of it and no more was anywhere to be seen on the horizon.

Nowadays, I get out of bed in the morning wearing a smile.

There is something about being awoken by a beautiful sunrise over the sea, just outside your bedroom window, and wearing flip flops and shorts in November that contributes to my smile.

By choosing the game of starting my own business, I have opened up a door that I did not know existed, to unlimited opportunities, personally, professionally and financially.

THE ROYAL WE

Emails have become such a convenient tool that one could wonder how people did business before them.

They have a huge role to play in modern-day business, but can also make more damage than good if written carelessly.

One day, I received this email from a company, with which I was discussing some project.

It went along those lines:

> *Dear Phillip,*
>
> *I have reviewed the agreement and I amended the document (attached) for your review. Let me know if it is ok.*
>
> *One the designs, I have looked into the psd and I think the resolution of 200 dpi will be ok, I tried a few combinations of design that I will send you later.*
>
> *Regards,*
>
> *Bob*
> *CEO*

Despite that misspelling of my name, to which I got so used to that I stopped paying any attention, quite happy just not to be Pierre or Eric for a change, I did realise one other important thing.

Bob was a very talented guy. He was the CEO of this company and by the looks of it, was also a lawyer and a graphic designer.

How many people do you think work in this company?

"Hmm...Bob is on his own", I guessed.

I guessed right.

One of the most underestimated things, and therefore too often forgotten about, is that everything counts. Every communication by email is as important as the big meetings or public presentations and needs to be given great care.

Bob's email had something in common with many other emails I came across, received from a CEO, President, VP, or Managing Director. It was saying "I have done this", "I have sent that", "I have prepared the contract", "I will check the problem" and so on.

By simply answering everything in so much details, Bob's email gave away that behind the "whatever nice title he gave himself" there was only a one-man band, or not far from it.

Bob's email would have given a much higher perception of his company if it had been saying "We have done such and such", "We have prepared the contract", "We have checked the problem", "We found a fix" and so on.

His email read as if Bob did everything and that perception was directly linked to the lack of dissociation between the person, who did something, and how what had been done, was communicated. It was missing a distance.

Let me rephrase Bob's email.

Dear Philippe.

We have received your comments on the agreement, which have been reviewed.

I am attaching for you the documents with some amendments. Please let us know if everything has been covered.

On the designs, our graphic designer (CC'ed) looked at the files you sent and confirmed that the resolution is ok.

Best Regards,

Bob Smith
CEO

Which email do you think works best?

Notice first that I have spelled my name right, which should not be a hard thing to ask, especially when you are trying to sell something to someone.

The dissociation between the owner of the company and the actions carried out is very important to make the interlocutor believe that the actions were not carried out by the owner himself, but rather by a team behind him, of which he is just the representative on behalf of his company.

A "We", "The team" or "My guys" or anything that is not saying "I", goes a much longer way.

Giving greater care to the phrasing of an email and the people involved in the communication, contributes a lot to the credibility and perception it gives about the company.

You are a CEO, so you must behave like one.

If you are seen doing everything, then you are seen as a one-man band.

And by the way it is OK to be a one-man band. Many people do great business on their own.

But if you have a company and you decide to call yourself anything else than the *Director* that you are, then letting other people see how much you are behind everything does conflict completely with the nice title you gave yourself.

A CEO, or President or VP, must create a real distance so that everyone seems to have a clear and consistent role within his organisation.

By the way, there was a time, when CEO used to mean something.

At the single mention of a CEO title, you could picture a Fortune 500 organisation with thousands of employees.

Nowadays, with the spread of internet businesses and the new generations of Start-Ups, the term CEO has lost of its credibility.

When I think about the first time I made a business card with the title CEO, I now laugh. I had a two days old company with one other shareholder and just four thousand euros in the bank account. I even had both CEO *and* Managing Director on a card.

For some reason, I continued making the same mistake for years, until I remembered one old advice from my first boss.

She only had Director written on her business card, and I asked her why she did not have Managing Director or something more significant.

She answered that by putting God on your business card you could not walk away from a negotiation as easily as if you were just a Director.

Basically, she explained that if you are God, then you are *the* decision maker, so why should you need to go back and discuss with other people before making a decision.

In contrast, when you are a Director, your interlocutor does not know how many other Directors are in your company, and while you are a senior staff, you can still easily walk away to reflect during a negotiation, as you are seen as one of a group of decision makers.

In her case, she was the only Director and *the* decision maker, but this trick helped her walk away, reflect and come back to negotiate stronger deals.

In other words, her view was that the God titles in a small business were more useful for the Ego than for business.

She was right, but it took me many years to realise it.

I cannot think of anything more ridiculous than a *VP of sales EMEA* job title in a company of three people. I have met a few such VP's and they were as ridiculous as they title.

Going back to the emails and the need to create a distance, you could get someone else to send some of your emails.

If you do not have anyone else, then you can just make someone up.

Without creating fake people, you can use generic emails when appropriate such as accounts@abc, support@abc, admin@abc, info@abc, cs@abc and so on.

Who is meant to know, who stands behind those generic emails?

Trust me, nobody will ever ask and nobody cares, but the communications look a lot more credible, when someone or some entity is included in the thread.

Why not also involve the other people, who are helping you?

For example, my friend John Smith is doing something on a project to help me, either for free (Yes! these people still exist), or for a small fee.

His help is completely punctual and he might contribute only very little and for a short period of time, but his biggest contribution is his first email.

I create an email jsmith@mycompany and I use it in all emails on related topics, either written from John directly or with John in CC.

The point is not to bullshit your way in your email communications, but just to be coherent and understand that an email from the CEO about sales, then from the CEO about accounts, from the CEO again about a marketing plan, then from the CEO about technical issues and bug fixes, then from the CEO about any other small things is damaging your credibility as a CEO and as a company.

I am confident that I can smell a one-man band by simply reading an email communication thread, looking at a business card or a website, and spending two minutes on Google.

Firstly, many are doing an awful job at it and have zero credibility from the first second, so anyone would see through it.

Others are doing a better job to be credible thanks to the little Potemkin villages they have built for themselves.

But I have been the one-man band, and I do recognise a Potemkin village, when I see one.

Becoming familiar and recognising a Potemkin, Inc. offers great advantages as well, by the way.

It also allows you to identify other Potemkin Inc. Start-Ups so you can carefully select the deals you want to enter into or walk away from.

In any case, using the royal "we" and spelling names right can only increase the perception you give to the people, with whom you are interacting.

ONE STEP AT A TIME

The impression of someone meeting you or at the simple mention of your name or your company is like a mental picture.

Marketing companies call it brand identity and make fortunes out of it.

This mental picture is dynamic and can change continuously with the circumstances such as your appearance, performance, media coverage, awards, announcements, rumours and so on.

Think of it as your reputation. It is people's perception of you and your company rather than a true reflection of your actual state or position.

It can change in an instant from positive to negative to neutral.

The Potemkin phase focuses precisely on that gap between the actual situation and how it is perceived.

The gap is especially wide for Start-Ups at the very start of their journey, when the product may not even be ready or well defined, logos are being changed every day and the website and business cards are still subjects of daily debates. In other words, the Start-Up is under construction.

When you are just starting, you do not want to be perceived that way, as you need customers and revenues. You need to give the perception that you are already open for business.

Whether ready for business or not yet, is secondary to your ability to control how others see you and your business. Getting the first step of "presentation" right is key.

Very often, I have seen fellow entrepreneurs pass on this first step quickly, thinking that they were wasting time on petty things and should get on with real business and close deals.

People, who rush the presentation step are not realising that it may be the step most worthy of their time and energy, and that getting it right will influence significantly the speed and quality of the deals that they will close after.

They forget that the perception that you are open for business plays a great role in closing deals.

Who would buy anything from you if they have the perception that you are not ready yet, or that they will be your first customer?

Nobody likes to be the guinea pig.

Taking care of how your Start-Up gets perceived from the very start is important, and that initial step of thinking about how you want to be perceived by the outside world, and what you need to do to achieve that perception, is often underestimated.

Let me tell you the story of Ben the bodyguard.

I once came across this single web page, which had created a motion of popularity so big that it ranked in the top 5,000 websites in the world in just one month, and got tens of thousands of Twitter and Facebook activity within weeks.

This was a "coming soon" web page, not even a website nor a product, just a parking page called benthebodyguard.com

Why was it so popular? Because the guys wanted to have the best parking page out there! The page was original, high quality, used latest web technologies and was intuitive to share with friends and spread the word.

This was an excellent Potemkin village that conveyed a great perception and a strong credibility without even having a product behind, just the promise of a product and nothing more.

They basically focused their efforts on getting the first step right and as a result freed some extra time to actually go and build their product, while this "coming soon" page was already working for them.

They eventually launched their product - although six months late on their original plan - and had a great head-start created from the buzz around their parking page and tens of thousands of people already aware of their existence.

I would bet that they had customers and partners lined up even before they opened the shop and launched their product.

I have often seen people neglecting the presentation step, and as a result, they ended up with poor websites that were not reflecting anything good about them, and with names way too long or inefficient because they did not bother thinking about a better one or doing some basic research; their business cards were useless and too easily forgettable; they had sloppy product presentations, and had failed to take the time to really think about their product and market, and to polish their slides.

Have you ever received a business email sent from something like companyname@gmail.com?

I do some times, to my amazement.

Is it possible not to see that receiving an email coming from a Gmail, Yahoo or Hotmail account kills completely the credibility of any company that you are trying to portray as open for business?

I am not talking about the email tools here, I am talking about the email address itself.

There is nothing wrong about using Gmail to read and send your business emails, I do it all the time and it has great tools to easily manage all your business emails in one place.

But not as a business email address.

You simply *cannot* be using anything else than an email address @yourcompany if you want to be taken seriously.

A domain name costs less than ten bucks per year, and a hosting package costs about the same per month and comes with email addresses and so on. So the total investment is less than $150 per year.

If you do not have $150 per year to spend, then I am afraid but you need to go back to the drawing board because you do not have a business.

It seems obvious that if I am representing a software company ABC Ltd., I would undoubtedly be better off by giving away a business card with an email @abcsoftware.com rather than abcsoftware@gmail or Yahoo or Hotmail.

I once read a quote that said to *take care of the seconds and the minutes will take care of themselves.*

I liked it, as it represented well the value of not rushing the initial steps and that the rest would follow automatically.

In the Potemkin phase, the initial step is about creating your company's image as well as your own image right, and opportunities will follow, like by magic.

Take a big brand like Guinness for example. They take their external image seriously. In fact, I would challenge anyone to find a pixel out of place or a bad quality image printed on an officially approved advertisement by Guinness in a magazine or a leaflet.

You won't find any.

Why? Because they want their beer to be perceived as quality beer so they focus on the quality of everything that represents their brand. They understood that everything counts and that if you sell quality, you must look like quality and Guinness is indeed perceived as a quality and original beer.

On the other hand, how would you feel if you came across the web site of a company, which seemed built by a ten years-old kid or built 20 years ago, with most links broken, and a layout all over the place?

It is fair to say that the poor look and feel, and the bad quality of the website, would put you off and affect your perception of that company.

Some organisations are so big that they simply do not think that everything counts.

"It's only a website", I have heard once.

I should have answered something along those lines:

> *"Wake up and smell the coffee old man!*
>
> *You may have a business worth many millions offline and have a good brand, but when I search for your company on the Internet, I have more chances of finding a garage or a porn site before I find you.*
>
> *And by the way, your website is so badly built that I cannot even look at it on my smart phone.*
>
> *Sorry if this comes as a surprise, but people are no longer using the heavy yellow pages book to find a business.*
>
> *Never mind, I just found your competitor in one click.*
>
> *Bye!"*

It would have made for a funny conversation.

A lot of established organisations do not put enough effort into their web presence because they are not realising how fast their business is changing. It used to be all offline, but now, they need to adapt and do it fast and well.

If they are not able to produce a quality website for themselves, which is nowadays perceived as easy and relatively inexpensive, how can I, as a customer, trust them to produce a quality product for me?

The same can be said of many companies, who carelessly let official materials go to print with distorted logos, faded colours, pixelated or cropped images.

How many pages can you write about your logo?

How about 150 pages?

I once came across an interesting document, which shows how much care can be put into what your logo looks like, how it is used, and where it is used. This document was 150 pages long.

Can you imagine 150 pages about a logo? More pages than in this book!

You would think it was a complicated logo, wouldn't you?

In fact, the document was the guidelines about the Swiss logo. You know the simple white cross in a red square logo.

I would recommend reading this document just to understand how much importance could be put into just a simple logo, which represents how we want others to perceive us and our business.

A 150 pages document is a bit extreme of course, but it helps reminding how much everything matters.

There is always a gap between what we are, and how we are perceived, and that gap can be influenced.

Depending on how well the gap is managed, you can create either a positive or a negative impact on your business.

In my first year in business, I had given great care about doing the first presentation step well.

Too well maybe!

It got me nominated for the Ernst & Young Entrepreneur Of The Year Award.

This is a very serious award. Some of the people, who won it, have revolutionised their industries, and many became billionaires.

How ridiculous was it that my one year-old business, which had turned over less than 50K, was in the same contest?

I decided to go through the motions anyway. There had to be something positive to get out of it, despite the fact that I had no hopes, whatsoever, of getting even just short-listed.

I did a long interview in front of a judging panel, and then waited for the evening ceremony, without really giving it any further thoughts.

As expected, I did not make the short-list, but as a nominee, I was invited at the Black-Tie ceremony, which in itself was an interesting experience.

I rented a smoking and went to the event in a luxury hotel in Dublin.

There was a good media presence to greet everyone.

I picked up a champagne glass on the way and started squeezing through the crowd to find my table.

I was sitting with all the other nominees in my category.

We greeted each other and started introducing ourselves and chit-chat.

The guy on my right had turned over 100 million Euros and the one on my left had 1,000 employees.

I was completely out of place.

Even though I had been nominated in the same way as they had, and none of us were in the short-list, we were clearly *not* in the same category *at all*.

This evening made me realise that while I had done the first step right, it was also *only* the first step.

These two guys were well ahead of me in their journey and there were many more steps to go in order to create a valuable business and come even close to any of those guys at my table.

While the Potemkin phase of a Start-Up focuses on the presentation layer that you create to give a more favourable and higher perception of your Start-Up than it really is yet, it does not mean that the Start-Up has to do nothing else.

It is not about being a pretty but empty shell.

The Potemkin phase just gives a boost, but it does not replace the hard work necessary to build a valuable business.

The positive perception created helps opening up business opportunities, which in turn enable the Start-Up to grow and reduce the gap slowly.

Eventually, it may become a successful business with a very small gap between what the company is, and how it is perceived.

When I look back at my own experience and that of other entrepreneurs around me, I am convinced that the ability to influence external perception, what I call the Potemkin phase in this book, is one of the most important factors in the success or failure of a young business venture.

POTEMKIN IN ACTION

The Potemkin villages can be figurative, like in some of my previous examples, but they can also be concrete physical constructions as in the following story, which shows a real Potemkin village that I have built to try to win a tender worth over one million.

My second venture was specialised in mobile data synchronisation.

We had a piece of software that allowed transferring data from one phone to another using some wireless technologies.

This was long before the iPhone made its first steps and the smartphones market was still in its infancy. Believe me getting something as simple as your contacts, from one phone to another, was not an easy task.

One day, I received an invitation to enter a tender for a large telecom carrier.

The carrier needed a system to transfer data between phones, for example contacts, images and so on, and move them from the old phone to the new one easily, at the counter, when people came to buy a new phone.

This was not something that we could do with our technology, but data synchronisation was such a niche area that the subtle difference between what was needed by this carrier, and what we had to offer, was understandably unseen by the person, who wrote the tender.

However, this large tender was a great opportunity and definitely worth answering.

Fortunately, I knew a company in Central Europe that was specialising exactly in what was needed.

They had not been invited to this tender process.

In fact, the carrier probably did not even know that these guys existed. They did not show in the Internet results and had never been noticed at trade shows or anywhere else that mattered.

This was a good example that our Potemkin Inc. was working.

We had been easily found and our presentation through our website, media coverage and the overall package did convey enough credibility to get invited to participate to this big potential deal.

This other company however, despite a poorer presentation, did have exactly the right product for this project.

I had used their product in the past and knew one of the guys in this company relatively well. Through him I contacted their CEO and explained that we had this invitation to tender.

I asked them if they wanted to answer it jointly with us, we would handle the communication with the carrier, who invited us, and they would provide us with their software in a reselling agreement.

Given that this project covered over a thousand shops and that this carrier wanted to move to other territories after this was proven successful in their home country, this was a very interesting opportunity for both that software company and for us.

The price tag for this deal was over one million Euros.

We agreed to partner and started answering the tender document.

We sent our detailed response to the carrier by the given deadline, and like most tender responses, this was a heavy document of over 200 pages, many appendices, spread sheets and so on.

We had worked very hard to give a quality answer, and objectively, I can say that it was a quality answer. We had understood the need and had offered a good solution for it, at a competitive price.

A few weeks later, we received an email saying that we were short-listed and were one of the handful of companies that were considered to become the provider for this project.

This was very good news, until the customer asked to come and visit our offices, as part of their selection process, in order to validate our proposition and allow us to move forward to the final two or three potential partners.

This is where the story became more complicated.

They knew that we were a Start-Up, but their perception was far from the reality. They thought that we were a medium sized company, with a dozen to twenty staff.

In reality, we were only two people at the time and were working from a fifteen square meters office.

In this case, we also were a simple reseller of another small company, miles away from us and whom we had never met.

How would we make this official visit a success and maintain their credible perception of our company?

We had managed, at a distance, to create a good perception through professional email communications and conference calls, and our quality answer to their tender request that demonstrated our expertise.

If their visit was a flop, we would lose this huge opportunity.

The challenge we were presented with was interesting and the Potemkin villages were our answer to it.

We contacted the carrier, organised the visit, agreed dates, and then started the construction field of our Potemkin village.

On D day, suited and booted, we waited for them to exit the arrival hall of Dublin airport.

We met, greeted and were on our way.

We had borrowed the car of my business partner's mum, a Range Rover Sport, to pick them up from the airport and add a bit to the first impression - and save money on a taxi ride.

Of course, we did not go to our fifteen square meters office.

Instead, we drove them to a business centre for Government sponsored Start-Ups.

My associate's brother had his offices there and agreed to prepare them as if they were our own.

We parked in the business centre, entered the back of the building from the car park and went up the stairs.

As we passed through the corridors to reach our meeting room, the customer was able to see a dozen people at work without any reasons to think that they were not our people.

On the way we greeted the actual owner of the place, whom we briefly presented as one of us, and continued to the meeting room.

A secretary came in to offer some coffees and we were set to start our meeting.

We turned on the conference call with our partner in Central Europe and with one of their guys based in the US.

This completed our plan to give the exact perception of our Start-Up as we wanted it to be perceived.

Not a one-man band, but not a huge setup either. Just the right size for this project, with a dozen people involved, well organised and in line with what we assumed the customer would expect to see.

Before we reached the meeting room, in the corridors, one guy had approached me. He needed to explain how the conference call kit was setup for our call. The others could not hear what we were saying to each other, they could simply see what it looked like, one employee discussing some matter with his boss. This added to the perception that we had created.

At one point, we had thought of putting our name plate above the name plate of the other company in the entrance, but in the end, I decided that the setup was sufficiently convincing without it.

We simply used the back entrance so that they would not get to see the main entrance of the building or start looking for our logo.

My associate's brother, who helped us prepare the offices, told me a story that in a similar situation, he had once pulled a trick and unlike us, he did stick his company name over another one with some simple duct tape.

My personal feeling is that there is a fine line between creating a Potemkin village for a positive purpose of seizing a business opportunity, and creating a set for a scam.

This was not a scam. This was our real business, something that we had given blood and sweat to create from scratch.

We were not trying to con anyone or steal anything, we were just trying to seize an opportunity that was given to us only because of the Potemkin villages we had built, and without which we would have never had such opportunity.

We were ready and had a very good product to offer. We just didn't have the staff or the offices to match it, yet.

Our meeting proceeded well, and we discussed everything that we needed to. The customer was happy with our answers, and all was going as well as it could.

During a break, I explained that we also had another office (the 15sqm one), where it had all started for us, and which I was still using because of its more convenient and central location.

Although a small office, it was located in one of the most prestigious areas of Dublin and happened to be very close to their hotel, so I suggested we got back there after our meeting in order to get closer to the hotel and organise the festivities for the evening.

We arrived to our "other" office. It was cleaned up and shining.

A few desks and a meeting table had been arranged to make the most optimised use of fifteen square meters possible and give a perception of space.

One of the desks was occupied by a friend of mine to whom I had given the keys and had asked, as a favour, to play secretary for the afternoon.

She spent the day on the internet doing her own things, while waiting for us.

When we arrived, it was already 5pm, so she greeted our customer, gave me a few envelopes, passed a couple of messages written on a Post it saying that such and such had called and then said goodbye, adding a little extra along the lines of:

"See you tomorrow. Oh, and remember that I have to do that thing in the morning so I will be a little bit late. Bye! Have a nice evening! Have a nice trip back!"

This was the cherry on top to turn our little grotto into a small but fully functional annex to the bigger office we had just returned from.

In reality, it was the only place we had and we were a few months late on the rent.

The pressure was high during the whole day, and we had to keep our cool to avoid any mistakes that late in the game.

The day was passing by and all was running smoothly for us. We knew our industry and the product very well, and we were delivering each answer with confidence.

At the end of the day, even though the product was not ours, this was our core business and we knew our subject inside out.

Later that evening, my business partner found a family excuse that required immediate attention and left us alone for the evening.

Although he swore that it was really so, I believe that he did not manage to handle the pressure for the rest of the evening and created an escape for himself, which I was not too happy about, but I could understand why.

We had to give constant attention to every single detail and every parole pronounced for such a long period of time, that it was exhausting.

Left on my own to handle and entertain the customers, I had to ensure that I concluded their business trip on a high note.

I brought them back to their hotel, organised the taxi for the next day to drive them to the airport, and then told them that I would pick them up one hour later to go for dinner.

The working conversations were over now and we were down to chit-chat and personal discussions. But I still needed to be very careful as not to let any awkward answers to some tricky questions asked casually, ruin everything.

We had done a very good job so far, and I was not willing to ruin our effort at the last moment over some uncontrolled chit-chat.

I had to remain focused during the entire evening, while at the same time, entertain, smile, joke and do all those things that make a dinner enjoyable and empty of silences and boring conversations.

There was a private club, which I was a member of for just twenty euros per month, and which I thought, would be the perfect place to bring them to.

This place was fantastic, it had three luxurious floors with two bars, a restaurant and a roof terrace, but most importantly it was for members only so getting a table was never a problem and you were looked after very well by the staff.

This was a little gem in Dublin that many Dubliners did not even know existed.

I had discovered it by chance, and was delighted when I had, as I used this spot countless times to discuss business matters. The place always reliably gave the right impression.

At the end of our dinner, we walked back to the hotel, saluted each other and the day was finally over.

I could finally begin to relax, and let the adrenaline go down, but I was too exhausted to go out for one drink and went straight to bed.

A few weeks later, I received an email saying that we had passed this on-site selection step and that we were officially in the final three candidates that they wanted to partner with for this project.

Unfortunately, about two months later, in a strategic reshuffle, the carrier considered that the project would no longer fit into the new plan and that the return on their investment would not be sufficient to push it further. The carrier cancelled the entire project and apologised deeply for having wasted everyone's time.

But our efforts had not been wasted, far from it.

This experience was invaluable and even Potemkin himself would have been proud of our Potemkin village.

In fact, we had already started to leverage on our participation in the tender with this huge company, even before the tender got cancelled.

We used the world-fame of the carrier to increase the perception of our own company.

Think of it this way. People would not think possible that a company could be selected by such giant potential customer and get short-listed, unless it was worthy of something.

So thanks to this adventure, other companies and potential investors automatically started to perceive our company as larger than it actually was, and new business and investment opportunities arose.

By the time the carrier cancelled the project, we had already closed another deal thanks to the credibility gained during our participation to that tender.

MUCH WANTS MORE AND LOSES ALL

Greed is the worst enemy of a one-man band with no money.

Some business owners are so focused on cost savings that they fail to invest in creating opportunities, which would generate revenues and resolve their financial crisis.

Greed *does not* close deals.

This is one thing that I have argued many times with former associates, and on many occasions I was proven right.

Greed, especially when you have little money, only delays deals, as it engages in endless negotiations, and often contributes to losing deals to less greedy competitors.

I believe that what closes deals is a good value proposition, well packaged, and well delivered. And by delivered I mean *delivered*, literally.

Not hesitating to travel to meet your prospects has on many occasions helped me close international deals.

The following two examples come to mind.

One morning, I received an email from a company in Europe, asking specific questions about our technology.

The questions were well-formed, and so accurate that I knew that the person, who had written them, knew the market well.

I took this email seriously, researched quickly the sender, liked what I found and replied to his email in detail, by lunch time.

We discussed over emails and phone calls for about a week.

The prospect wanted me to do some consultancy work worth about ten thousand euros for just a few days of brain picking, some research and a document to write.

The prospect approached other specialised companies or other individual consultants, but they failed to find many suitable candidates for this particular consultancy job.

This was a very particular field, a bit outside of our core business, but in which I had a high expertise, but most importantly I had responded quickly to their initial questions, and then created a positive momentum over precise and prompt email and phone communications.

They started to look at me as their solution.

I was less expensive than the others, had a flexible approach to the terms and was already proactively giving them information and ideas to resolve their problem. They had no doubts that I knew my stuff.

The truth was that I needed some revenues very badly.

One deal had just fallen through, another one was hot but slow to come to life, and the few invoices that I could collect from, were not due for another two months.

I was in between things, with some time in my hands but in desperate need for money.

We went quite far in the discussions, and what was missing now, was simply to get that deal closed.

Feeling that this deal was just waiting for someone to bring a pen along, I decided to take action.

I called them proposing to fly over for a couple of days, go through the requirements in more details with them, meet face to face and prepare everything needed to start the work as early as the following week.

I proposed to do this out of my own money, and we didn't have a contract signed yet.

They agreed.

Of course they did! There was no risk for them.

If they liked me, they would give me the project, and if they didn't, they could walk away easily. There were no strings attached.

I borrowed some money from a friend to pay for the flights and accommodation, and I went.

Our working session was very fruitful, we bonded well and I flew back with the deal signed.

I had borrowed 600 in order to seize an opportunity to make 10,000 based on the belief in my ability to close that deal face to face.

The other shareholders did not want me to go because they focused on the 600 that this would cost rather than the 10,000 that this could bring.

I remember them saying that we could not afford *gambling*.

But it was not gambling. It was taking action to close a sale and investing in resolving our temporary financial crisis.

There had been a lot of work to bring that deal to a boiling hot point and I was convinced that it simply required someone to give it a push.

If someone does something for you for free, don't you feel obliged to return the favour and do something for them if you can?

By taking initiative and flying over on my own expenses, the prospect saw confidence, and did not have the feeling that I was doing it just for the money, but that I also was genuinely interested in helping them make this project a success.

Unless something dramatic happened, he would have absolutely no reason to deny me the deal in return.

And this is exactly what happened.

In fact, a few years later, the customer told me over a beer that he had already decided to give me that project just after I proposed to fly over on my own expenses. The commitment and confidence that it transmitted had closed the sale.

On another occasion, I received a similar email, but from Asia this time. It was well-written as well and came from a serious company.

And this time, it was also asking *precisely* for our product.

I answered the email promptly and further emails and conference calls followed.

For an entire week, communications went back and forth and the deal became hot.

This project had specifically tight deadlines for delivering a customised product for a telecom carrier.

Work needed to start very quickly and distance was becoming an issue to close this deal.

The prospect was based in South East Asia, and while we sort of agreed on the deal verbally, I did not have a written acceptance yet and we had not started exchanging any paperwork.

I started thinking about this potential customer, who was in an exciting market and wanted exactly the product that we could give him.

We had to close that deal.

The deadlines were very tights and to make it happen, the development work needed to start *yesterday*.

Feeling that distance was the only issue to bring this deal home, I decided to remove the distance from the discussions and booked a flight to Singapore.

I would get this contract signed there, face to face, and save a lot of time in a time-sensitive project.

We are not talking about a short hop between European capitals. It was a rather a long and costly trip to Asia. However, I did not need to borrow money this time, as I had the necessary funds available, I just did not have enough customers. This was a perfect opportunity to get one.

I organised the trip that afternoon and was on my way.

My associate was not even aware of those exciting conversations. It had happened so fast, and he had not been in the office for a week.

I let you imagine his surprise when he called me on Friday, saying:

"Hey I'm back! What are you up to this weekend?"

And heard back that I was on my way to the airport to fly to Singapore to close a deal.

But thanks to my initiative, once again the prospect saw confidence and a company without particular financial problems.

The prospect also saw the kind of responsiveness and proactivity required in such type of deals, where timing is critical.

To take the opportunity to close that deal, I had paid for my flights and accommodation out of my own money, without a contract or any guaranty to close that deal.

Do you think that after that, a serious prospect could make any non-sense excuse not to sign the contract or not close the deal?

Of course not!

I flew back with the contract signed in my bag, and the prospect became a customer, and later became a friend and more business followed.

These were just two examples that greed is an enemy when the company is in desperate need for money, or customers.

It is a risk of course, but a risk controlled by the high quality of the work performed prior to creating the opportunity.

Is entrepreneurship not all about risk-taking, anyway?

And is money not relative?

I believe that it is not about how much you have, but about what you do with it.

I have often felt embarrassed, when looking at how much more I was earning, every month, compared to many of my friends.

However, they were as happy as Larry, and had a lot more to show for than I did, because their expectations were in line with their income. They did everything they wanted to, within that range.

You can earn just a couple of thousands a month and be completely fulfilled, while others can earn tens of thousands per month and still manage to struggle to make ends meet.

Let me ask a simple question.

Do you think that someone could make a billionaire feel poor?

I do not mean the *inside* wealth or *it's the nice person that you are that makes you rich.*

I mean: Could someone make a billionaire feel poor? Literally!

My initial answer to this question was "probably not", but then I heard this story that proved me wrong and made me rethink entirely my approach to money.

It was an eye opener.

The person in this story is someone, whom I came across and admired a lot. Perhaps, if he recognises himself, he could contact me and give the version from the horse's mouth.

The story goes that this Irish billionaire was playing golf at one of the very exclusive courses in the US.

He was teamed up with some younger Indian guy that he had never met before.

Wealthy people playing in those kinds of clubs always have a bet on the game and the bet usually ranges in the tens of thousands of dollars.

This Indian guy asked him how much he wanted to bet, expecting the usual ten, twenty, or even fifty thousands, whatever the standard was.

Allegedly, the Irish guy arrogantly answered that it didn't matter because he was worth over one billion.

So the Indian guy answered:

"OK! You're on!"

He intended that he was ready to bet the entire one billion on that game.

This answer set the Irish guy back a little. This was his entire fortune.

The Indian guy was actually worth forty billion. That was forty times more than the Irish guy.

Put in perspective, it means that if the Irish guy had lost, he would have lost *everything* he had, while the Indian guy would have still had 97.5% of his fortune left.

The Indian guy was joking of course, but I bet that it made the billionaire feel poor, even if just for a second.

You would think that he was in an unbeatable league being worth one billion, yet someone came along and had a lot more.

So money *is* relative.

Going back to investing in closing deals, when you have little money, being greedy is counter-productive.

The little amount of money you try to preserve so carefully only stagnates and eventually slowly disappears without having done any good.

When a business has little money, it needs to create revenues otherwise, it just slowly dies.

I could think of a few more examples, but I am happy to say that the success rate of my non-greedy approach to closing deals is 100% to-date.

GOOD DEAL, BAD DEAL

A business mentor once taught me to always walk away from a bad deal, no matter what.

In fact, he was right, not all deals are worth entering into.

The difficulty is that when in financial need, people tend to see every deal as a good deal, because they are in need.

I got bitten back too many times to remember for not walking away from bad deals.

Although I knew that they were bad, I needed them in order to resolve a financial struggle.

"What is a bad deal?" you may ask.

A deal could be bad because you failed to smell a one-man band behind the deal and that particular one-man has not been able to deliver on schedule, and with the quality required.

A deal could be bad because the financial terms are too long, or the cash flow does not work for you, or you made some mistakes in your calculations by underestimating costs or overestimating revenues.

The risk analysis is an important part in any deals and many forget to give it enough attention or refuse to see the worst case scenario.

In my experience, the worst case scenario is often the only scenario, at least at the start.

I once worked all the way through the nights, every day, for nearly a month, in order to deliver a German version on my software and a customised website.

What I had failed to see was that this was a bad deal from the start.

It was a - *do all the work for free, and once it is working, we will share all revenues* - kind of deals.

I had focused on the potential revenue-share, blurred by the relatively big customer I was partnering with.

I had failed to see that there was no marketing initiative and no concrete plan to push the product, once ready.

In fact, none of the obvious questions were asked, so none were answered, and the revenue-share of zero, even a good share in your favour, remains zero.

And to make things worse, I even started this gigantic work on the back of a non-binding MOU, not even a contract.

This rookie mistake bit me back, when the project never went live, and I wasted all this precious time and energy.

But making this mistake and a few others, did serve me well in the end.

I learned my lesson and began to better structure deals, ask the right questions, make the right calculations and ultimately become a better business person.

Working for free to put something on its feet can be fine, when there is a concrete benefit in doing so.

In the previous example, I had not only miscalculated many things but I had also forgotten to factor in the cost of my own time.

I had been working for free for so long that I actually forgot that my work also had a value.

Even if you decide to get it done for free, you must factor in the value of the work done.

The customer did not have the perception that what had been done had any special value at all. It seemed like a standard setup.

In fact, it was my own fault in this case as I had sold it well that way in order to close the deal.

When I actually started doing the work, it turned out to be much harder, and longer, than I had thought, and all this effort was given away as a free gift.

A piece of advice is to always carefully assess the work involved, but most importantly to always make clear in any deal, the value of the effort involved, whether you charge for it or not.

I found that it is acceptable to everyone that nobody works for free.

Here are some examples and variations of a similar deal to illustrate how creative a deal structure could be.

Imagine that a customer wants to buy your product, but you need to customise or install something before it goes live, and that the cost of this setup is estimated at 10,000.

For the sake of this example, let's say that you agree with the customer that after the setup costs are covered, you will share all revenues at 50/50.

This is a simple deal, where the customer pays you 10,000 to get everything ready and then you share equally the revenues collected.

Imagine now that you want to get more revenue share.

You have two ways to do it. You could negotiate a 60/40 split, and go into all the justifications about why this split in your favour would be fairer.

Or, you could also transform the deal structure into a setup cost worth 10,000, but given free of charge, but a 60/40 revenue share in your favour, thereafter.

In this case, giving the setup worth 10,000 for free is your justification for the higher share of revenues after.

There are also other alternatives to this deal.

Imagine that the negotiation is getting tough and the customer does not want to move from the 50/50 split.

You could offer the setup worth 10,000 and give it for free, like in the previous example, and agree on a revenue share of 50/50 to make the customer happy. But make the 10,000 cost recoupable to you.

This means that the first 10,000 of revenues that will come in will be for you. The sharing will only start afterwards.

The other way around would also work.

You could charge the customer for the 10,000 setup cost, but make it recoupable to him.

This means that you would receive the 10,000 up front and when the revenue-share starts, you will get nothing until the revenues to share reach 10,000.

In other words, you give the customer his money back on his initial cost, when the revenues start coming.

There are infinite ways to structure a deal.

These were just a few examples of course and each deal structure fits a particular need on one side or the other.

Experience and practice helps creating deals that both parties are happy to sign. But remember that factoring in the value of everything that comes out of your pocket is important, even if it is your own blood and sweat, and even if you give it for free, it has a value.

Giving a value to my own effort has helped me many times in structuring better deals with real win-win models.

Being knowledgeable about numbers is a great asset for any business person, and for a Potemkin, Inc. entrepreneur it is an even greater asset that helps transmit more credibility and business acumen.

If delivered well, the creativity of the business models you propose, and your ability to handle the commercial part of a deal can increase seriously your own credibility in the eyes of your customer, who will appreciate dealing with an experienced business person.

For a while, I was untouchable on my business plan for all the technology aspects of my project, but I knew that I was weak in the numbers, and lacked experience and accounting jargon to handle advanced conversations with investors, banks, venture capitalists, and experienced business people.

I had to become more knowledgeable with numbers, and started to study accounting to better understand the financial aspects of business, until I realised that there was a better, and more efficient way, than just reading books.

I hired an accountant to go through my business plan and polish all my financial spread sheets.

What I did not need, was someone, who would just do the job and send me the results along with the bill.

I needed someone, with whom I could work closely side-by-side in order to better understand and familiarise myself with all the terms used, all the numbers, and how they all related to each other.

In other words, I hired him to get a crash-course in accounting based on real numbers relevant to my business.

Thankfully, I soon became a lot less vulnerable on my financial projections and could have a decent conversation with any accountant, financial advisor or business owner.

This not only increased the credibility of my business, as my numbers were a lot more realistic and I could back them up better, but it made me more credible as a business person.

I could feel a drastic change in the level of conversations I was having with financial and business people from then on.

FLYING FREE

In previous chapters, I told stories and anecdotes about the difficult times, but thankfully, a Start-Up business is not only about financial struggle and offers many Ups as well.

Thinking about some of the memorable moments during my journey, I am still not sure if I am happier about the first time I saw my photograph in a national newspaper, or gave my first interview to a business magazine, or if waiting for a flight in the swimming pool on the roof of Singapore airport, or sky diving over Sydney before going to a meeting made me feel better.

I work long hours and have many commitments that I must meet, but I always have a smile on, because I am truly enjoying doing what I always wanted to do for a living; working for myself with all the associated freedom and satisfactions.

I think my smile comes from feeling free and in control of my life.

I am currently living on an island like I said I would years ago, when I started in business.

It's not quite Fiji, but as I am writing this chapter, I am sitting at a café by the beach with a mojito beside me, the sun is shining, and I am wearing flip flops and shorts in November, so I cannot complain.

The high moments of my entrepreneurial journey not only influenced my business positively but also gave me a great boost to continue following my dream and believing in my projects.

After a few articles in the newspapers and magazines, I realised that many high moments could be used to your advantage, when they are in the public eye.

Reviews in serious media, award nominations, significant milestones, partnerships, signed deals, and so on, all convey a lot of credibility to the external world about both you and your business.

Believe me, letting people see an international business that has an award-winning product with over one million users, and has many world-class customers and partners, does positively influences my current business conversations and opens up business opportunities.

There is no need for Potemkin anymore then, you may think, or is there?

Well, Potemkin is needed for as long as the gap between reality and perception of reality still exists.

I may have a business with attractive numbers, some additional shareholding here and there and a lot of ideas, but I have not reached my dream yet and neither am I wealthy.

In fact, with four mouths to feed, I must give constant attention to creating new stable sources of income and therefore, still need Potemkin to help me create new opportunities and leverage on all the achievements to-date in order to convey the necessary credibility to create more.

As you grow and achieve valuable things, the gap automatically reduces and building big Potemkin villages may not be needed anymore, but the odd Potemkin houses here and there are always needed.

I can say that I am enjoying the entrepreneurial journey, and living the dream is not only about financial stability, it is also about personal satisfactions and freedom.

Over the years, I have met many people in business, who did not like me as a person. I was too French, too this, too that.

But I can comfortably say that most of those people did respect my work ethics and no one could say that I did not know my stuff.

Likewise, I have seen many people and even done business with some, whom I did not like as persons, but I had respect or even admiration for certain of their abilities or achievements.

If you are speaking to a self-made man, who built a multi-million fortune out of an ice cream van, or a billionaire who started an empire in his garage, or even an eighteen year-old, who wants to set up an airline and does it, you cannot have anything else but respect and admiration, regardless of whether you think that he is a nice guy or not.

Business is business, for the most part. Sometimes it does click, and I have occasionally made some friendships out of business relationships, but most of the times it does not, and it does not matter.

They do not have to like you, they have to respect you and vice and versa.

I have focused my career on trying to do, what I do, well, and I must say that seeing your work appreciated by your peers is part of the high satisfactions of an entrepreneurial journey.

But none of it would be the same without the freedom of having fun along the way.

I have had the chance to travel a lot thanks to my choice of work, and travelling is one the things I have enjoyed most in the entrepreneurial life for the many cultures I got to encounter, all the sorts of people I met, all the troubles, and all the fun.

A business can come and go, but the travels create a personal baggage that you continue carrying with you going forward. They impact your life positively, way past your current business adventure, and all the way through the next ones.

Having fun while doing business does keep a smile on your face, and makes the ride more enjoyable especially when times are difficult.

A few years ago, in mid-January, I was catching up with people after the long holiday break. They had all just gone back to work and were getting ready for a new year.

My year had already started about two weeks before. In those two weeks, I had taken fifteen planes and been in seven countries.

I counted fifteen because one of them was one-way only, as I jumped out of it enjoying my first sky diving experience.

Six month later, I did the same again, but this time I was in Australia for a week of work.

I woke up at dawn, went to the centre of Sydney and signed up for a sky dive that same morning.

This was an amazing experience and a great feeling of freedom.

Not the freedom of falling from the sky and pretending to be a bird, but the freedom of being able to jump from 5,000m in the early hours, then take a bus back to my apartment, change into my suit and tie and go to the office.

The freedom of being able to do whatever I wanted to, without having to ask anyone for permission.

On a few more occasions I have felt that freedom of being an entrepreneur and working for myself.

In Singapore this time, I was not meeting my customer until late that morning. I flagged a cab to go to the zoo. I had breakfast with the monkeys, flirted with a gigantic python and saw rare white tigers. Once breakfast was finished, I took a taxi and went to my meeting.

When I had to fly back home a couple of days later, I went to wait for my plane on the roof of Singapore airport, drinking cocktails in a Jacuzzi by the swimming pool.

What a way to wait for your flight, let me tell you.

I believe that having fun is an important part of the Business persona you are trying to communicate to your customers.

And is also an integral part of the Potemkin phase, as it creates a baggage of stories and anecdotes that you can tell during dinner to fill some uncomfortable blanks and get people to remember you positively.

I remember one such week in Kuala Lumpur, Malayisa.

We were a team of three and had flown to meet with a customer to discuss budgets and also teach their employees about our technology.

The week had been long and intense work-wise.

On the third evening, we decided to relax and have a drink to take some of the pressure off.

We went to a bar with a colleague and with our Chinese customer, with the goal of making him discover Mojitos.

We did achieve our goal. He discovered and liked Mojito, probably even a bit too much.

We were having great fun, talking about casual things and joking like a group of friends.

At one point, I pulled a deck of cards from my bag and started showing some magic tricks to my customer.

I used to travel with my cards and magic props everywhere. I had been interested in magic and card manipulation since I was a teenager.

I must say that I have not found a better way to break the ice, yet. Apart maybe from taking a Rubik's cube lying on a shelf in someone's office, completing it and then putting it back without saying anything, just waiting for the person to realise half-way through the meeting that it was completed and wonder how it was possible.

That evening in Kuala Lumpur, I began warming up with some basic magic tricks involving cigarettes and cards and then worked my way up to some more advanced and impressive mind-reading, vanishing cards and levitating objects.

Asian people are a good audience and their reactions are priceless because they often genuinely express surprise without social filter.

We laughed a lot and this worked well to reinforce the bond with my customer, with whom I am still friend to this day.

The bar staff also liked my performance and started to gather around the Mojito drinkers' table to look at magic tricks all night.

That night, I have done every thick I knew. I was exhausted.

The next day we went back to the bar and the bouncer greeted me saying:

"Good evening Black Magic!"

People's perception of a good evening is as important as their good perception during the meetings.

In fact, it may be more important because you discover people outside of the business context, you casually exchange more personal views and you create a stronger bond.

This opens up more opportunities later and also makes the conversations a lot friendlier, as from that point on, future arguments around numbers and percentages can be handled with smiles and jokes instead of more serious fights and mind games.

This makes business better and faster and as a result frees some of your time.

I used to fly to Asia quite regularly at some stage and on one occasion, as my business trip was coming to an end and I was about to fly back to Europe, a good friend of mine wrote me an email.

He had landed in Hanoi to wrap up his six months break around the world and was going to hang around in Vietnam for a little while.

My flight back to Europe was scheduled in the next few days, so this was short notice.

But I did not need to call anyone or ask for any permission. I only had to think about it by myself and correctly assess the work that had to be done, and prioritise things accordingly.

I changed my flight back to Europe for two weeks later.

A couple of days later, I flew to Ho Chi Minh City and met with my friend and his cousin.

We spent the next two weeks holidaying in South Vietnam and Cambodia, enjoying local food and customs, shooting with AK-47, eating happy pizza, drinking beer, smoking Alain Delon cigarettes (only French people would get how funny this is) and having great fun in general, taking a well-deserved break from my daily business meetings and entrepreneurial life.

My business did not die and I managed to get everything done.

I simply prioritised things in a way to allowed me to be away for two weeks and continue running my business, sitting at Internet cafes, from time to time, to read and answer emails, and making a few phone calls, when required.

That freedom was priceless, and is undoubtedly the most valuable thing I got out of running my own business.

JUDGING A BOOK BY ITS COVER

One particular Saturday afternoon, over ten years ago, we had gathered with a group of friends in the basement of one of Dublin's many pubs to half-watch a rugby game on a giant screen, and half-socialise, drink beer and discuss various topics of interest.

Most of us were foreigners, who had arrived in Dublin a year or so earlier to ride the Celtic tiger wave of prosperity that Ireland created in the late nineties.

We were all working in a business park, either in IT or in finance.

Like most foreigners, who came to Dublin back then, we had been recruited for our language skills by giant firms, which had set up their European headquarters in Dublin.

Our conversation moved from gossip to jokes to nonsense back to jokes, and eventually turned to our personal lives.

We started talking about our past, before coming to Ireland. Where we were? What we did?

My turn arrived and I started recalling my time in Kazakhstan just a couple of years earlier.

Back then, my life was very different.

In a nutshell, I had a five-star lifestyle and a serious consulting job in the oil & gas industry. I was flirting with the strategic subtleties of the Caspian Sea region, was involved in import/export of various goods and was part of the international business world in Central Asia, where frequent traveling, embassy receptions, and meetings with government officials were part of my daily life.

This contrasted a lot with my friend's previous lives and most importantly contrasted a lot with my current one, which they were part of, and knew very well.

I was not a business person at all. I was a supervisor in a financial company.

As I started to explain how I had bribed a custom officer with a poster of Zinedine Zidane, I could start to see some sceptic looks emerging.

When my story reached the point, where I got kicked out of the country, I had lost half of my audience.

I could see some interest, but scepticism was taking over and they thought that I was joking and just taking them for a ride.

The cover did not match the book at all.

Before I tell the story, just remember the circumstances. We were all in our mid-twenties, wearing simple casual clothes, drinking beers in an Irish pub in Dublin and having fun.

Here goes the story.

In my early twenties I got a job in Paris for a small French consulting firm that was acting as a middle-man between French companies and companies and governments in the former Soviet Union.

This consulting firm sent me as an expatriate to Almaty, Kazakhstan.

This was long before anyone knew this country, later made famous (or infamous) by Sasha Baron Cohen's character Borat.

I'll skip the details to go straight to the evening in question.

One evening, I received a phone call inviting me to attend a private party organised by a minister and his wife to celebrate the birth of their grandchildren.

I had just travelled 600km by car that same day back from Bishkek Kirgizstan, so I would have gladly given it a miss. But they were a nice family and I could not refuse their invitation without offending them, so I asked the driver to drop me home, showered, changed and went to the party.

Although a private party, this was a relatively formal party with half of the country's most important people invited, including some ministers, business people, members of the presidential family, and famous cultural figures.

Thankfully, this was not my first time attending these sorts of events, and I had learnt to become relatively at ease.

Those types of dinner had extremely long tables with guests seated by hierarchy of importance. I obviously was sitting at the bottom end of this long table, reflecting my low importance among the guests.

In fact, apart from a few high-level foreign guests from UNESCO, I was the only foreigner. I was invited as a friend of the family and knew most of the local guests personally, so I freely interacted with everyone along the long table, but my seating was clearly positioned at the bottom end.

A live local band was entertaining the crowd with some Kazakh songs and the guests were dancing and having a good time.

Following a very bad advice from one of the guests, I accepted to offer an innocent dance to one of the daughters of the President, who looked very bored at the corner of the dance floor. We had already met once on a previous occasion.

The President's son in law happened to be the head of the Kazakh oil business and was the third most powerful man in the country, whom many bet on becoming the President's successor.

So when I felt a hand on my shoulder, and turned around to see the angry look on his face, I had to think fast, very fast indeed. I stepped back, smiled, and put her hand into his hand, as in to pass him the relay baton, and walked away.

The party continued, and a few hours later I went back home, tired, but in a good mood, after what I had thought had been a nice party.

I had had a good time, and I barely recalled the dancing incident, it had been so insignificantly brief and small in my mind.

The weekend passed and on the Monday, I received a phone call from a trusted friend. He explained to me that I had to follow his instructions fast, and that he would explain later.

I was not to go to my client's office, from where I usually worked.

Instead he asked me to leave my apartment, leave money to pay any outstanding bills, flag a taxi and go to the small apartment that we were using as our registered office, where he would meet me later.

I was a bit confused by what he was saying, but fully trusting the source of the advice, I obliged.

In just two days, all my working conditions had been cut from the very top down and I could no longer even talk to anyone in business, and by *anyone* I mean *anyone at all*.

Only some faithful few had understood that this was a case of what Russians typically call, *making an elephant out of a fly*.

Leaving my building, I spotted a couple of black tinted-window cars with government plates in my car park, which seemed a little too much out of place for my liking.

I left from the back doors and flagged a taxi.

I spent the rest of the day over the phone with various people, annoyingly listening to stories about how the elephant was growing bigger and bigger by the minute, like a bad Chinese whisper.

As the hours passed, I started to look at it with humour and tried to guess what the next story was going to be.

By noon, some singer's wife had been added to the story, by the afternoon, I had sex with her, and by the evening, I was an addict, and had drunk an entire bottle of vodka and bothered every woman present.

Listening to all this was driving me crazy.

I knew for a fact that I was not drunk, as I had gone easy on the drinks, limiting me to the mandatory shots of vodka during the important toasts.

I certainly did not give a crap about the President's married daughter and I had absolutely no idea who the fuck the singer's wife was.

In my analytical mind, I was trying to rationalise what was happening, until I realised that there was nothing to rationalise.

All of these allegations were invented, and blown up to ridiculous levels without rationality.

I felt like a famous rock-star, reading made-up gossip headlines, except that I was not famous, and barely existed. I was confused about who would benefit from all this hassle to me, or the company I represented.

In the evening, I received a phone call from the most influential person I knew in Kazakhstan.

If he could not resolve this, nobody could.

He told me frankly that this was coming from too high for him to do anything, without putting himself into trouble as well.

When he added that I should also be watching my back, I decided that this wasn't worth the hassle, and called it quits.

He organised a flight for me that same night leaving for Moscow in the early hours. I never returned to Kazakhstan.

In the plane, while sipping some whiskey, I debriefed the past few days. Everything happens for a reason, but the reason for what happened there, remains unclear to me to this day.

But I must say that I was surprised not to find all this as much disturbing as I found it fascinating.

Effectively, at age twenty two, I had been kicked out of a country for an insignificant two minutes dance.

This made me smile as I was thinking at the long way that those new countries born out of the collapse of the Soviet Union still had to go.

I returned from Moscow to Paris for a face to face with my boss.

To this day, I still don't know if she believed my version or the others, but I'd like to think that she did believe me.

I obviously lost my job, although it had not been put to me that way in an attempt to be nice.

Here, I finished my story.

I could see the extreme confusion in my friends' eyes growing.

They were obviously expecting me to burst out laughing and tell them that this was a joke and I had invented it all.

This is understandable if you think that most of the people, who listened to my story had not done much with their lives yet, and we were all working in a completely different environment now, which was so distant from my previous life that it made it hard to believe that what I was saying, was relating to the same person that they knew.

Yet this story was true in its every details, and the moral of this anecdote, is that what you wear, who you are, how you behave, all that you are perceived to be, must match, somehow, what you are telling, in order to be taken seriously.

Although they guessed that this story was true, because we were good friends, and there was no reason for me to lie to them, they still struggled to switch off their image of me now, and picture me in the lifestyle and environment of this story.

It was only later, after seeing some photos of those days, hearing other stories relating to that period, and seeing me in more formal business situations that they started seeing it differently and managed to turn off their current perception of me.

They eventually did believe my story.

SOCIAL COMPLIANCE

One of the things I have not yet elaborated on in this book is the more psychological aspects behind the Potemkin approach.

People have one weakness, out of many, that particularly makes their perception more easily controlled.

People tend to comply with defined social rules too easily.

The concept is simple and it even has a name, *social compliance*.

Our society has a number of predefined rules that people have preconceived ideas about, and that are anchored so strongly that people rarely question them.

By understanding those social rules, and applying them, I realised that people simply complied, without asking themselves some very basic questions.

For example, if you look like a doctor, behave like a doctor and speak like one, people will perceive you as a doctor, and will rarely question what they take for a fact.

The following scam works for that very reason.

I know what you think. I should not be using a scam to illustrate my example, especially after having spent most of this book trying to explain that Potemkin, Inc. entrepreneurs were not con artists.

It is true, but what is also true is that social compliance is the greatest tool of a con artist, and the psychological reasons why it works in scams, is the very same reason why the Potemkin villages work.

This scam illustrates better the psychology behind social compliance, than any other example that I could think of, in a business context.

Picture a woman fainting in a restaurant.

One of the customers is a doctor, and offers his help, to the relief of the panicked waiter.

The doctor pulls some tools out of his bag, and starts checking the woman's eyes and breathing, and all the things that you usually expect a doctor to do.

Everyone simply sees a doctor saving a woman.

What they do not see, is that the doctor is saving the woman behind the counter, and that while he is asking everyone to stay away to let her breath, and sends the waiter to the kitchen to bring her a glass of water with some sugar, he frees himself some space to take the money from the counter, and put it in the woman's bag.

He then simply carries her to his car, because of course, her condition is serious, and he must drive her to the hospital urgently.

The waiter even helps putting her into the back seat of the car, and is relieved when they leave.

Everyone in the restaurant is still a bit shaken by what just happened.

Gradually the shock disappears, and the waiter realises that the day's earnings are gone, that the doctor was a fake, and the woman his accomplice.

In a situation like that, it would never come to mind to ask the doctor for a proof.

He said he was a doctor, looked like one, spoke like one, and even had tools like one. This was proof enough for the waiter, and the customers, to just comply.

The same applies to police officers.

If you wear a uniform, or any distinctive piece of equipment associated with law enforcement, and if you behave like a police officer, and speak like one, why would people actually question the fact that you are a police officer?

They have no reason to do so.

It would not come to the mind of many people to ask a police officer for identification, would it? Even though this is completely allowed by the law, and even recommended by the Police itself, when in doubt.

These examples are just some of the stronger categories socially complied with, but guess what?

The same applies to business people.

If you look like a businessman, and behave like one, you create some opportunities associated with businessmen.

These could go anywhere from airport lounge access, business class upgrade, free internet, favours of all sorts here and there, all the way to huge deals with some of the largest corporations in the world.

Over the years, I discovered that a businessman belongs to a social category, highly complied with.

I cannot count how many times airport staff, cafe staff, hotel staff, waiters, operators, other business people, and administration staff just *complied*.

I looked the part, spoke the part, and there was no possible doubt in the mind of my interlocutors that I was the part.

Taking notice about what you wear, how you speak, and how you behave, helps you guess how you will be perceived, and whether this perception matches how you need to get perceived in order to achieve a particular goal, whatever that goal may be.

I often took great care of those aspects before meetings in embassies, consulates, and various administrations, because I knew how much the bureaucratic machine could waste in precious time and energy.

Whenever I played the social compliance card right, I immediately saw the quality, and efficiency, increase considerably. I even felt myself growing a few inches, and started feeling the part, not only looking it.

I have managed to get certain complex administrative things done in record time, and with a smile, despite some expert people telling me how impossible it would be.

I recall a yearly business visa being prepared on the spot, while I was sipping a cup of tea upstairs, with the economic advisor and the consul, discussing opportunities in their country, instead of the usually, less pleasant, waiting and *service* through pretending the customer does not exist, so common in former Soviet countries.

A friend of mine also comes to mind. He had been battling with the immigration department about a mistake on his documents, and asked me for help.

For nearly two years, assisted by a solicitor, he could not get it changed, no matter how many letters they were sending explaining that there was a mistake.

I saw a hole in his approach, and advised him on how Potemkin would have proceeded.

The top guys were not the right interlocutors and letters were not the appropriate way. In fact, the more junior staff behind the counter was more likely to make the desired changes in the computer, if forced to comply in the right way.

He was sceptical, but had nothing to lose, so he executed my plan.

On Monday morning, he went to the immigration counter, dressed like I told him to dress, speaking like I told him to, and doing everything that I had advised him to do, precisely.

I picked Monday for the dizziness that follows the binge drinking weekends that Irish people enjoy so much, and that without doubt, some junior public servants of the immigration office had enjoyed as well, thus becoming the perfect *target*, for that very reason.

Ten minutes later, he left the building with a brand new residency card, with his name modified, and his nationality changed.

He was delighted, and his solicitor was gobsmacked.

Playing on social compliance not only made many of my business dealings, and travelling, much more enjoyable, thanks to the greater quality of how I got looked after, and the generally good mood it creates, but most importantly it also created strong business opportunities, as the first people to comply with a credible businessman, are other businessmen.

NO MONEY, NO HONEY

When you are starting in business, you have two ways to do it, with or without money.

If you decide to do it on a low budget, like I did many times, then you enter into what is called bootstrapping.

Bootstrapping is a common term used to describe the launching of a business on your own with a low budget. It implies outsourcing most of design and product development, renting equipment, and usually means having no real office, and no salary.

It is a valuable way to get started, and enter into the market fast.

With the Internet in particular, this process is made easier, and has become very common practice.

It has risks of course, because you are outsourcing most of the work, so you become dependent on someone else to do what you have in mind.

Most failures are due to poor communication with the outsourcer, especially when communicating your requirements.

It makes sense, if you think about it. If you are not precisely telling someone what you want them to do for you, how are they supposed to know precisely what to do?

If in addition, you keep changing your mind continuously, then you are making the work of the outsourcer even more difficult.

After having got outsourcing wrong a few times, I understood that agreeing on specific terms, giving precise and final requirements, and having a contract that all parties were happy to sign, did prevent many issues down the line.

I have always been comfortable with bootstrapping, maybe more by necessity than by choice, but many people prefer to go for a safer strategy. They ask people for money to back them up before starting a business.

After all "no money, no honey", as they say.

I went the fund-raising route many times, and I found it hard, because until I became experienced in it, I consistently underestimated the timings and outcomes of the funding process, and shifted my focus, from running my business, to filling some countless spread sheets instead.

Raising funds is a full commitment for a prolonged period of time, onto an extremely bureaucratic road. It can affect both your work and personal life, because both depend on the success of your funding round.

In my last experience of it, I stopped counting after version 32 of the same spread sheet with forecast projections.

As you may have already noticed, I dislike the VC and other similar types of funding processes.

Not because it is hard, but because I think it is full of shit for a large part.

I managed to raise funds at various stages, and completed a number of formal funding rounds, but I am still not comfortable with the process itself.

Making a business plan is ok. Thinking about your market, your product, how it will fill a need in that market, and having a strategy to sell your product, and so on, is all OK.

You must do your homework before you start a worthy business, and that is completely necessary to have any chance to succeed.

But being asked to project your business over five years from now, with details, as precise as, how much will come in and come out, every month, for those five years, makes no sense to me whatsoever.

I have made many spread sheets, and have seen many spread sheets of other businesses, and not one of them, not one, was in line with what happened, just three months later.

Investors need to know that you have a serious plan, that you can put a number on how much your business may be worth investing into, and you have an idea of the planned returns on their investment. And that's fine.

But young Start-Ups, or just seed ideas, have no clue about how many customers they will get in week 27 of their projections.

This is way too far to mean anything.

So people invent numbers. That's what they do.

I did it, I saw other people do it. Many may not admit it, but believe me, they did it too.

The numbers may be rational, have some logic behind them, and make complete sense from the outside, but they are usually just based on a formula, whatever the formula is e.g. x amount per month for the first year, then x increased by y per cent for year 2 etc...

It means absolutely nothing!

The reality is that, any external factors, can rewrite those numbers in an instant.

Think about the arrival of the iPhone, and how it revolutionised forever the mobile industry, in just a few years. I bet that it forced many businesses to go back to the drawing board with their five year plan.

My issue with the value of those numbers thrown on a spread sheet, is not only about the time wasted in preparing them, but is also about the fact that because they are invented, they can randomly go both ways, over or under estimated.

You plan two customers per month and you end up getting six, so all is good, you may say.

In fact you just gave away 45% of your business to someone, who invested on the basis of two customers, and you just quickly tripled his worth, while he did not triple his investment.

Or you plan two customers per month, and end up getting two per year instead. Your business struggles. You had built up your expectation, based on a spread sheet that you started to believe in yourself, but was worthless.

Spread sheets should only be guidelines. There is no reason why an investment into a Start-Up, or a seed idea, should take nine month to complete.

I am not saying it should be impulse buying, but not far from it.

It is a risk that can be quickly calculated, and the investment should be based on that risk.

Why waste nine month, and make the business struggle financially, while it is waiting for your "potential" money?

As a direct consequence of this long and uncertain process, the business cannot perform to the level of the numbers forecast in the spread sheet during that time, because it has no money, and the focus is shifted on filling spread sheets, making presentations, and pitches, instead of running the business.

The debate could be long on this topic, but I made my mind up, and I prefer the DIY approach.

Maybe I have been unfortunate, or maybe the process is really flawed for some types of young Start-Ups.

I once went to a VC meeting. This was a respectable VC organisation, with a strong reputation, and so on.

The financial guy did his part well, and I enjoyed talking to him.

He even spotted a couple of interesting holes that I took note of, fixed, and reused later in the next version of my spread sheet.

The other guy, an old technical consultant of some sort, was responsible to assess my business from a technology point of view.

I had done this many times. I knew my stuff inside out, so I was relaxed and confident that I could handle a grilling by a world expert on the topic.

It became clear very quickly that this guy was no world expert, not even close to an expert in fact, to the point that I even wondered, if he knew how to turn on a computer.

He asked me the most stupid questions, in the most patronising - *I know it all kid, I am the expert* - kind of way.

I was boiling inside, as I had hoped that this VC meeting would finally lead to an interesting opportunity to put my business on its feet. Instead, I was here, listening to the non-sense that this guy was throwing at me.

First, I gave him a chance. I thought that I should consider his remarks, thinking that I had maybe missed something, until I realised that he had no clue whatsoever.

My business was too technical and too niche for this guy to understand it.

He struggled to swallow his Ego, and simply ask me specific intelligent questions, like many other, more prepared VC's, had done in the past.

Instead, he went on a technology name-dropping monologue.

I interrupted the guy politely, and shook his hand. He shook mine back, surprised. It had gone too fast for him not to spontaneously respond.

I then shook the financial guy's hand, and simply said:

"Thank you for your input, it was very valuable, however, this guy is insulting my intelligence, and I am sure that we both value our time enough as not to waste it. Thanks. Good bye!"

I left the room, and walked away.

Between shock and surprise, I managed to see a smile on the financial guy's face, indicating that I may not have been to first guy to have been fed up with the other guy's crap. I may have been the first one to walk out though.

I believe that the funding process is for certain types of people, and I am not one of them.

I like concrete stuff and snappy response, rather than fume and hope on a long tail.

A good friend of mine has gone through the long process with a particular Venture Capitalist, and got dumped at the last minute by SMS, not even face to face.

The entire alphabet of bad words has been used to describe this investor, and to this day, the F word continues to be added in front of his name, whenever he gets mentioned.

Another friend of mine, however, went through this entire process as well, and received a few millions in funding.

This helped him a lot grow his business that he later sold, and made a lot of money out of. He now invests in other businesses.

I am not killing the funding process in itself, it obviously has a value, and having money helps a lot, but I would question its coherence with the daily reality of a young Start-Up.

If you have ever tried to raise funds for your business, then you have realised that it is hard to attract any investors, until you have already an investor interested.

But as soon as one investor becomes interested, then the others seem to follow, like by magic.

This chicken and egg situation is understandable, if we look at the basic psychology behind making a decision, and assessing the risks of spending money.

Before, spending money, people tend to look to the behaviour of others, in order to give some value to something.

If everyone is buying it, then you are thinking that you should be buying too, but if nobody is, then it is a lot harder to make the decision to be the first one to buy.

To get out of this chicken and egg situation, good old Potemkin gave me a solution.

I started by raising small investment from credible entities, like government agencies helping small companies, and Start-Ups.

I also put money in myself, as the investment of your own personal funds shows your commitment, and belief in your project.

Then, I started building Potemkin villages to present those small investments in a way that made them perceived as much more relevant, than they actually were.

Because of the perceived lower risk that previous investments had transmitted, it rendered the decision of bigger investors, such as Venture Capitalists, Business Angels and banks a lot easier.

I have applied this approach a number of times with success.

Realising that I needed to raise money to seriously take my first venture anywhere, I started researching every funding for Start-Ups available in my city, and in my region.

I found one that could not exceed five thousand Euros, and was intended to help Start-Ups build a proof of concept.

This was funded by the government, as part of a European initiative to drive entrepreneurship, and help in the initial phases of the business.

The reality was that five thousand Euros was nowhere near what I would need to make it happen.

I had a business plan asking for several millions of Euros, but nobody, in their right mind, would give me millions just like that.

So I decided to turn on the Potemkin machine.

I met with the government agency, filled all the forms, and prepared everything necessary to get this small funding.

As soon as I received it, I immediately added the logo of the Government agency to my website to increase its credibility, and give a perception of some sort of affiliation with a respected authority.

Other potential investors I spoke to afterwards, began to look at my business plan, and investment request, more seriously, knowing that someone had already put some money in, and knowing that the government assessment procedures, were usually long and detailed.

Having been approved was, in itself, a good sign that the business had potential.

But I did not leave it there. As soon as I was allowed to, I applied for another grant, in another field, and received that one as well.

This helped me increase further the perceived credibility of my business, as the government did not only invest in my idea, but it did twice.

Larger potential investors started to think that I must have a good idea, if someone else took the risk twice already.

I leveraged on everything, no matter how small it was, in order to control the external perception about my project, and get more.

This overall increased credibility allowed me to close further more important investments.

I eventually managed to pass many due diligence processes to finally convince a government agency to invest over half a million Euros in my business, and become a shareholder.

Despite my dislike for the funding process, I have relied on it a lot, and learned many valuable lessons along the way.

Lesson number one was that *a deal is not done until it is done*, and lesson number two was that *timeframes are always longer than expected*.

I burnt myself many times, while learning those two lessons.

For any investment into your business, you must think in terms of six to nine months before you have any money available.

This is a very serious mistake, which unfortunately many young entrepreneurs dive into, to underestimate the real time needed to close a financial investment transaction.

If it takes anything less than six months, you are lucky, and it is likely to happen only with private individuals, investing in your business.

Any form of investment from an organisation of any kind, will take longer, and I am ready to take bets with you on this.

I have gone this road way too many times, and fallen into the trap of underestimating the timing required to see the money actually reaching my bank account.

I failed to understand quickly that an investment deal agreed, and a deal signed, can have months between them, and that the same applied for the time between a signed deal, and the money sitting in your bank account.

This is why, on a good advice from a fellow entrepreneur, I have started to less worry about having more than one egg in my basket, and rather worked on having more than one basket instead.

ENJOY THE RIDE

Many entrepreneurs get quickly overloaded with work, and do not find time for anything else.

In fact, this is a dangerous phase of entrepreneurship that can damage familial and social life a lot.

I have broken relationships, and have also seen many others lose their marriage, and companions, over their work.

The truth is that someone starting a business tends to get overloaded with fake work, especially when times are hard.

They fail to prioritise correctly, and they do not distinguish what is urgent, from what is important.

They become simply so passionate about their company, or their idea, that their work becomes the only thing on their mind.

I know it for having made this mistake numerous times myself, and having seen many others, make the same mistake too.

The solution was simple. It was not to take yourself seriously most of the time, and simply give an impression of seriousness, when required.

Being able to switch, from serious to fun, did help me enjoy the process, and stay in touch with reality.

With my feet kept on the ground, I simply became a nicer person to be around with, rather than the constantly busy, or distracted, friend or companion.

Let me tell you a story about a photo that was published in a national newspaper, alongside an article about me and my business.

That evening, I had received an email from a newspaper for an article that they had written, and for which, they needed a suitable and high-quality photo to publish.

I was excited.

The journalist needed it in the morning, in order to meet the deadlines for going to print.

Luckily, my house mate was a photographer, so I thought that I could easily get a photo done that evening, or first thing in the morning.

At that time, I was sharing a wonderful house with a friend of mine, Tim, and we used to spend every night playing video games or watching movies projected on a giant screen that we had set up in the living room.

That evening, we got carried away and at around 2am, I realised that neither of us would wake up early the next morning, and that I needed to get that photo done now.

We were half -drunk, very tired, and it was late, but I had to get this out of the way quickly, or I would miss the newspaper's deadline.

Luckily for me, my friend was such a good guy that he did not mind helping me take this photo, even at two in the morning.

While he went to take his camera, I went to take my suit, a shirt, and a tie.

I started thinking about a suitable background, and surely, a mountain of empty Carlsberg beer bottles, was not what was required for a national newspaper.

I decided to go for a portrait photo, which I felt could be done much faster than a full body shot, and required less preparation.

I turned on my computer, opened up my company logo, and made it as big as I could onto a full screen.

It was going to act as a background for my portrait photo.

Because this was a portrait photo, I did not feel the need to bother with trousers, and was still in my boxer shorts.

I did not iron the shirt either. I simply wore a suit jacket over it.

My friend shot a dozen pictures that we looked at on the computer.

One photo stood out, so we selected it, and I sent it by email to the journalist, at about 3am.

The next Sunday, I proudly came back home with the national newspaper under my arm.

The article had been published, and the photo was on half the page, showing me and my logo in the background.

It looked and read very well, and nobody, until now, could have ever imagined in what conditions we had taken it.

Nobody could possibly have access to that part of the story.

In fact, what everyone saw was that my business was in a national newspaper, with a half page spread, and nothing else.

I will let you imagine how much easier my business conversations, and sales have been in the weeks that followed.

My friend's name also appeared in the caption of the photo as credits, so essentially he was in the national newspaper too.

We had fun, and laughed a lot about it that day!

Many people would take an article in the national newspaper too seriously, and may stress or waste an entire evening, probably ignoring their families, just in order to take and send a good photo, on short notice to meet a deadline.

In fact, taking it easy and having fun worked just as well.

It's only an article after all, and sending a suitable photo is not rocket science, far from it.

Letting loose and relaxing in the process makes the journey a nicer trip.

CONCLUSION

I hope that you have enjoyed reading my interpretation of the Potemkin villages, and the stories and anecdotes that I have selected to illustrate the Potemkin phase of a Start-Up.

I have tried to make this first book original and personal, so that entrepreneurs at various stages of their journey could relate to some of the situations that I have described, without having the impression of following a typical "how-to" guide.

Some of the views I have shared were my very personal views.

I can expect that while some readers may have agreed with them, others may have disagreed. But I would like to think that all have enjoyed the personal touch that I have tried to give to this book, and have kept entertained.

The Internet Era, the social media craze, and the digital world in general, are making possible for Potemkin, Inc. Start-Ups to turn an idea into a successful business.

If you have taken just one single idea, or read one thing that could help make your business better, or enjoy your entrepreneurial journey more, then I am glad you took the time to read this book.

Putting across that the Potemkin phase was not a ruse to fool people in negative ways as in politics or in scams was not easy.

The Potemkin phase plays a far more positive role and is a building block that enables a young Start-Up business to comfortably handle questions such as "Who else is buying from you?", "Will you still be around next year?", "How many customers do you have?", "How many products have you sold already?" or any of the other very common questions that I have heard frequently at the start of my entrepreneurial journey.

Hopefully, you understood that Potemkin, Inc. entrepreneurs are neither thieves nor con artists, just business people going after their dream, finding creative ways to give a favourable perception in order to create opportunities, which may be unreachable otherwise.

By being able to create opportunities in ways that are not taught in any business schools, they manage to efficiently boost their business out of its seed phase and get out of the chicken and egg dilemma that they are often confronted to during the first deals or investments.

By inventing their own 80/20 rules, Potemkin, Inc. entrepreneurs learn to take greater care about the twenty per cent that other people see, rather than worrying too much about the eighty that they don't, and have fun doing so.

APPENDIX 1: ON THE WAY TO THE BEACH

I believe that understanding the author's journey, both personal and professional, does help the reader get more out of a book.

For this reason, I decided to summarise some main events of my own life, in order to better put this book into context. Adding a chapter as such would have only bored any uninterested readers, but this Appendix seemed like a good compromise for the others.

I was born in Moscow of a French father, ex-military officer, and a Russian mother, a translator from Moscow.

My upbringing was made multi-cultural, both by my family background, and by the troubled suburbs of Paris, where I made my first steps.

By suburbs, I do not mean residential suburbs with nice houses and gardens, but rather sky high cement semi-ghettos where countless nationalities try to live together in the confined space they have been given.

One half of the people living there is not integrated at all, and frankly do not even seem to want to, rather content to be living off social benefits, and taking as much as they can, without ever giving anything good in return, while the other half struggles to integrate itself, more or less successfully.

Like many kids, I started as an excellent student, but as I reached troublesome teenage years, my focus shifted, and my studies started to move up and down.

My mother always wanted to give me a good education and made every sacrifice possible to get me accepted into one of Paris' most praised schools, the College Condorcet, which was a real turning point in my life.

A year later, I joined another prestigious high-school, the Lycée Carnot, where were educated many famous alumni including former French president Jacques Chirac, several ministers, philosophers, aristocrats, and a Nobel prize winner.

Needless to say that this new educational environment, where classmates were belonging to families of chief executives, police prefects, Counts and Countesses, and internationally recognised figures, was a drastic change compared to my previous far more ordinary classroom.

I had to constantly navigate between two worlds; a suburb in crisis dominated by lower class, social issues, and violence, on one hand, and a luxurious Parisian environment surrounding me with culture, wealth, higher class and aristocracy, on the other.

It was both challenging, and stimulating, to get simultaneously accepted by both ends of the social spectrum.

My daily commuting between those two worlds was long, and at times dangerous. I regularly had to defend myself against petty theft, and once got badly stabbed, just half an inch away from spending the rest of my life in a wheelchair, or worse.

But as a result of those frequent changes, I believe to have developed an ability to rapidly adapt to fast-changing external factors, which forged what one would describe as a "street-smart" kid.

I completed my studies in Mathematics and Physics, and entered into University studying the same.

In parallel, I took a short detour by the military, where I voluntarily enrolled into a one-year training programme run by the Air Force commandos, and spent all my weekends, and holidays, in an army base, playing with boys toys, and training to become an officer. Although a very enjoyable period with some memorable moments, I never did anything with this military training after having graduated from it, with mention.

I have also enjoyed University, but my campus times were brief and I left early, disillusioned by academic perspectives, more eager to discover the working world, and earn a living.

I got my first job in a publishing company, selling advertising spaces door to door.

Back in the nineties, this sector was dominated by the Jewish community in Paris, and was reputed for being mainly run by confidence tricksters, with border-line business practices.

After a few months, I discovered that this reputation was indeed founded, and while this was a priceless school for whoever wished to become a con-man, and make easy money, this was not such a great school for someone interested in getting a serious job.

I then started doing some freelance interpreter work, helping Russian business people trading with the Parisian fashion houses.

Through that Russian circle, a combination of circumstances got me a dream job.

I began working as a consultant, liaising between French businesses and those of the former Soviet Union block, which later got me to move and live on my own, in my early twenties, as an expatriate to Central Asia.

This experience was undoubtedly a crash-course in international business and foreign affairs, with a front-row seat into the subtleties of Russian business, including everything that new independent Republics born out of the broken Soviet Union had to offer, from Russian mafia to corrupt officials, rogue businessmen, extortions, and much more.

It is in this environment of oil, gas, gold, minerals, fashion, and criminals that would be best described in an Ian Fleming novel, that I learned, without realising it at the time, a lot more about business, than any business school could have ever taught me.

My job in Central Asia allowed me to discover the highest levels of society, and to regularly deal with top business people, politicians, and embassy representatives.

It helped me improve both my English and Russian language skills considerably.

In fact, my English was already good, but my Russian lacked contemporaneity, because I used to speak it mainly with my mother. Slang was completely unknown to me and I did not even know the F word, before I moved to Central Asia. I caught up quickly though, and by the time I came back, I knew the entire Russian slang alphabet.

This was a nice period of my life, and my first experience of real travel, freedom, and wealth, which I rediscovered only ten years later, in the Start-Up world.

All good things come to an end though, and so did this experience, cutting short the nice career in Russian business that I had started to picture for myself.

I went back to Paris, looking for something new to do with my life.

I had to put behind the five stars lifestyle, the oil rigs of the Caspian Sea, the international business world, the embassy receptions, the meetings with government officials, and go back to the reality of the Parisian suburbs in turmoil, where people's interests were limited to clandestine dog fights, robberies, smoking hashish (preferably in non-smoking public areas), cowardly picking fights at ten against one, and vandalising cars.

I found it very hard to fit back into that shitty environment, so I decided to spend most of my time in Paris, living with a good friend of mine, who had a studio apartment by the Louvre.

A few months later, the International Chamber of Commerce organised an exam in Russian business studies. It was opened to University graduates, but also opened to independent candidates, who could demonstrate an equivalent work experience in Russian business. I believed that the field had taught me a thing or two, so I enrolled.

I passed this exam relatively easily, and received a diploma that I gave to my mother, delighted to immediately add it to her souvenir files. This piece of paper was not resolving my problem of finding a job, but it made my mother happy.

Working in France did not excite me, and the perspective of living in the suburbs had become a complete turn off, so I started looking abroad.

In 1999, attracted by the booming Irish economy, I applied for a job in an American company based in Dublin. A few weeks later, I left Paris to settle in Ireland, where I had planned to stay for one year or two, and eventually did for over ten.

After a few different jobs, I settled in a managerial position that stimulated me. It was well paid and involved a lot of business travel. I made many friends in Ireland, and enjoyed the Irish way of life.

In 2005, empowered by the Celtic tiger, I took the crucial decision to leave the stability of my managerial role in the corporate world, risked all my savings, and set up my first business.

I was full of energy and pumped up by this newly started entrepreneurial journey, which made me discover an unprecedented liberty, and control over my life.

I got to meet some of the most influential business people, had my photo in the national press and magazines, and was nominated for an Award as *Internet Entrepreneur*. The Irish government gave me some financial help, and later assigned a well-respected mentor to guide me through the early steps.

All seemed to be like the entrepreneurial life I had dreamt of.

In reality, none of this really helped in getting anyone to trust a rookie with no entrepreneurial track record, asking for three million Euros.

No matter how good my business plan was, I soon ran out of money, and never managed to get the necessary funds to concretise my first project.

Instead, I sold my services to a company that was working on a similar idea. This was a win-win situation, for me to get out of my difficult financial situation, and for them to get someone to lead their project.

This company was like a pool of entrepreneurs that step-by-step took me under their wings, and gave me an invaluable insight into Start-Ups, and business in general.

Despite my failed first venture, I continued to be energised by the process. I understood that I had managed to get some things right in my first attempt: I had managed to build and convey enough credibility about my business idea, and myself, to be taken seriously, and as a result created a motion of positive events and opportunities that would change the rest of my life.

That closed circle of entrepreneurs made me discover this exciting world that I wanted to be part of, and I then realised that I had reached a point of no return into the corporate world.

Indeed, just a few months later, I got another idea, and set up my second venture, providing mobile synchronisation software to mobile operators and service providers.

I ran this new company for four years, and managed to bring it into the attractive, yet difficult, South East Asian market. My Start-Up was recognised among the most promising high-potential Start-Ups in Ireland, I was among the nominees for the coveted Ernst & Young Entrepreneur of the Year Award, and I convinced various investors including the Irish government to take part in my business and become shareholders.

So far, so good?

Not really!

In 2009, as we were about to receive half a million Euros from a funding round, the story took a darker turn.

A series of frictions with my business partners emerged and lead to another point of no return, less enjoyable this time.

Tired of running the company single-handedly and getting little if no support from the other shareholders, I openly discussed my frustration with them. Their response made me realise that I had lost control over my own company. Key decisions were too easily overturned by the controlling 51%.

I decided, with regrets, that I would be better alone than badly surrounded, so I resigned from my CEO and managing director positions, and left behind everything that I had given my blood and sweat for, and had built from scratch.

My resignation broke all relationships, personal and professional, with my former business partners, who started to panic. Not knowing what to do, they chose the legal route.

I received a letter from their solicitor threatening to sue me for nearly half a million Euros.

In addition, all customers and suppliers I had worked with, and knew personally, started calling to inform me that they had received a letter warning them not to engage in business with me anymore.

The truth is that most of them had found this approach utterly unprofessional, remained faithful to me, and eventually also broke up their relationship with the company. But the consequences of this bad move had gone way above the heads of my former business partners, who simply went into attack mode, as if I had suddenly become the public enemy number one.

These attempts to damage my reputation pissed me off and I hired a well-respected, and equally well-paid, solicitor to fight them back vigorously.

After a long legal battle that finally got settled in my favour, I received some compensation and was set to move on with new ventures, and leave this mishap behind.

I then started a mobile software business called SafeBox, followed by various other projects never too distant from web and mobile technologies.

In just a year after I started, SafeBox had already attracted one million users, and won the Mobile Messaging Award 2011 for Best Messaging Application for Consumers. Safebox is set to become a successful venture.

During those entrepreneurial years, I spent most of my time in meeting rooms, airports, hotels and travelling the world trying to bring my business ventures onto the international scene.

After some time spent in Italy, adding the Italian language to my arsenal, I eventually moved to Asia, where I could finally enjoy living by the beach, like I had always wanted to, and watch my kids grow and enjoy a lifestyle that I did not have when I grew up.

In the past couple of years, I have been toying with a few ideas. I chose some and took action to make them concrete.

Some of those ideas, like SafeBox, are becoming successful, others are fading out, but I continue taking action on my ideas, with the firm belief that if nothing is ventured, nothing is gained.

This entrepreneurial journey, while chaotic and full of compromise, has been the most valuable period of my life.

Anyone, who knows me, would tell you that I have always been a man of ideas, but these few years have been an eye-opener for me. I discovered that ideas without action are nothing more than a waste of brain power, and learned how to take action efficiently to turn ideas into concrete opportunities.

Not short of mistakes and disappointments, my entrepreneurial journey reinforced my trust in the structured principles lying behind success, and ultimately enabled me to do now, what I always wanted to do for a living, be an entrepreneur.

APPENDIX 2: THANK YOU FOR SEEING

Although I have always had a huge admiration for Steve jobs (1955-2011), I was not planning on writing anything about him in this book.

Sadly, his death coincided with my writing, and after reading the many comments and debates on whether he was a genius or not, had invented anything or not, and the overall techy battles I was expecting, I started reflecting on his impact on my industry, my business, my ideas, and where I was right now.

I had not really reflected on it before, but it made me realise how much I did actually owe him.

I decided to write a brief thank you to recognise his positive impact on my entrepreneurial journey. In fact, he probably deserves a tremendous thank you for seeing what consumer wanted, and giving it to them in ways that changed forever how we interact with our mobile phones.

A friend of mine used to always refer to him as a genius. I would not quite agree on canonising him after his death, but a true *visionary* is about right, from my point of view.

I am not a hard-core iPhone or a Mac user, although I have used them numerous times for either work or pleasure.

On every occasion, I have been amazed by those objects that he proudly presented and represented.

Their simplicity was outstanding, and so were the user experience, the aesthetics, and the clever use of technology.

Anyone, who has used an iPhone long enough, cannot take another copycat in his hands, and not think about how far it still has to go to become as good as the iPhone.

Because of my line of business, I can appreciate Steve Jobs' achievements especially in the mobile space, rather than the never ending Mac vs. PC battle.

For me, he has revolutionised the mobile industry, in which I operate, by "inventing" the concept of Apps and App stores, opening up the market for touch screen devices, and overall for making mobile technology a very fashionable thing that can get any non-techy person excited, from a kid to a granny.

As I was reflecting on the iPhone specifically, I also realised that the way it was perceived by people around the world, had something very relevant to the message I have been trying to convey in this book.

I would not go as far as calling Apple a Potemkin, Inc., given its several hundreds of billions worth, but if I look at the iPhone alone, as a product, there is something fascinating about the gap between the reality of the phone's real market penetration, and how people perceive it.

We are talking about a phone with a small global market share of a few per cents, yet everyone thinks that everyone has one.

If I ask anyone, anywhere, about the iPhone, people know about it, have one, have had one, want one, have seen one, touched one, or had something to do with one.

Marketing dollars can buy a lot or things, but achieving such gigantic and global perception, and driving such an irreversible trend of new generations of phones, is just outstanding.

I believe that Steve Jobs' contribution to my industry, and as a direct result to my business and my person, has been invaluable.

My hat goes off to salute you for the vision that made such an impact on how people see and interact with their mobiles and rendered possible to create a viable business out of just an App.

Rest in peace!

ACKNOWLEDGEMENT

Over the years, I have met and interacted with a lot of people, whom I could acknowledge in this book for their impact on my entrepreneurial life, and indirectly on this book.

However, listing here the obvious people that have been part of my life until now, such as friends and family, would serve little purpose.

They know, who they are, and how immensely grateful I am to them.

However, I have selected a short list of people that I would like to acknowledge here, for the value they added to my entrepreneurial journey, either directly or indirectly, and to their knowledge or not.

Brian Tracy and **Jack Canfeld**, whom I would acknowledge together for having both, had a similar input. They shared their huge expertise of the principles lying behind success and sales, making me realise that there were some defined rules that if followed, could achieve specific outcomes consistently.

Brian Tracy's course on sales and sales management, put in practice, got me, in one single month, a sales commission pay check six months' worth.

President Bill Clinton, who needs no introduction, and whose path I had the pleasure to briefly cross, in one occasion, during a good friend's wedding, in a luxury hotel on the west coast of Ireland.

The immediate charisma of this man is notable, and it was interesting to see how his presence influenced the crowd. In this case, the crowd was made of a dozen of drunken Irish wedding guests running after him in the corridors, trying to shake his hand, while abusing his secret service guys with jokes way too sarcastic for them to truly understand.

Timothy Ferriss, bestselling author of "The 4-hour workweek", whose freshness and interesting view on outsourcing your life has had a good impact on how I manage my time.

Owen Fitzpatrick, International Trainer and Practical Psychologist, co-founder of the Irish Institute of Neuro-Linguistic Programming (NLP™), author of "Not Enough Hours", bestseller in the Irish book charts, and co-author of "Conversations with Richard Bandler".

I have the pleasure of being friend with Owen. He is a great guy, whose approach to life is extremely interesting, and every time we have dinner or simply a pint, I come out of our encounter empowered and motivated. "A big thank you for sharing your experience with me and helping me fine-tune this first book!"

H.E. Paul Romanovitch, former French ambassador to Kazakhstan and Kirgizstan, with whom I have learnt to understand the subtleties of geopolitics and who, by being delayed in one occasion in Kirgizstan, has unwillingly forced me to improvise a way out of a very delicate situation, during an opening ceremony with the city major, the region governor, some journalists, and many business people.

I learned on that day that you can be left on your own to either swim or drawn. That day I swam, thankfully, but pumped up by the adrenaline, I may have given him more abuse than needed, when he finally arrived. This was clearly out of line, given our respective positions, but it made me realise that behind title, no matter what these titles are, there are normal people.

I used to be impressed by titles, but after a while, I started to give titles a lot less importance than to the person, who stands behind them, be it the cleaning lady or the President. In fact, I met genius people behind crap titles and complete idiots at C levels.

France's former consul to Thailand, whose name I do not remember. He comes also to mind, and deserves a special mention, as his refusal to help me one day, resulted in me being stuck in Bangkok airport without any money, for potentially a week. I eventually got my way out of that stressful situation in three days, and now look back at it with a nostalgic smile.

Back then, smiling was not an easy task, given that I had to improvise in order to find food, keep from boredom, manage my sleep, keep clean, keep a positive attitude, find ways to communicate and adapt to my interlocutors, and of course, do all of these things for free, as I did not even have one single Baht.

Valekhan, a man of all trades, whose ability to navigate between each sides of the law I found fascinating. He has been my valuable "umbrella" in Kazakhstan and has helped me in too many occasions to remember here. He made me discover the beautiful post-Soviet ways of customs and excise that could be tenderized by a simple poster of Zinedine Zidane.

He made me understand the reality of issues with gangsters (Russian, Chechens and others), cops, corruption in general and all those things that I only had read before in the media or seen in movies. He made them very real for me, and I can only thank him for that eye opening opportunity that no business school could have possibly given.

He also made me discover a different angle to what social responsibility could mean, when playing football every week with some street kids in Almaty. He is a great man to whom I will always be grateful for having watched my back under all circumstances, and until the very end.

Sholpan Kulmahanova, business woman and wife of the former Mayor of Almaty, Kazakhstan. We met through a connection with her daughter, whom I have been doing business with in the fashion retail industry. We once had a meeting to discuss a business opportunity in the medical equipment sector. This meeting has been one of the most valuable meeting encounters I can remember, because it made me truly understand the value of perception.

She initially thought that I was a translator because I was there with my boss, whom she knew and respected, but who didn't speak Russian. As a result, she treated me with the utmost disdain for half an hour. I could have been the waiter for all she cared. Being young and a bit short-fused, I got pissed off by her attitude and our meeting soon turned into an open raw to clarify my role and what I was really doing there.

This memorable raw got me kicked in the legs by my boss a few times under the table, while I was vigorously fighting my ground trying to get accepted for my true role at this meeting, which was not that of a translator, but rather of the person, who was going to lead this new business opportunity.

This encounter made me realise the importance of perception, of what you wear, how you wear it, what you say, how you say it and that every details count in creating an impression. Whether this impression matches the one you want to give depends on how well you look after those details.

Ahmed Y. Mestoev, adviser to the Prime Minister of Kazakhstan. Our meeting was brief and late at night, to discuss some business opportunity.

This meeting made me realise the dynamics of the various hierarchies and the associated perceptions. This guy was the adviser of the Prime Minister, not the Prime Minister himself, yet you had the feeling that you were having a meeting with the President.

The intensity of the meeting was intimidating but a great lesson on little tricks to be taken seriously.

Maryse Makarevitch, French business woman and an extraordinary person, who has shown me what being goal-driven really meant. She was in her sixties, when I worked for her, and despite her age, she was always the first in the office and the last out.

This woman was a sponge of information. She had this incredible ability to dig into tons of information collected over the years and always pull the accurate piece of data in any situation. Although she was old-school and drove her business with out-dated tools, due to her generation, she was nonetheless doing business at an international level with extreme success.

I realised alongside her that the things that really mattered where knowledge and expertise, or at the very least, giving a perception of knowledge and expertise. I remember her first assignment for me was to read a ton of books about Central Asia and remember as much as I could. Thanks to working for her, I have learnt to become a sponge too.

Rashid Sarsenov and **Gulnara Sarsenova**, husband and wife, some very influential business people in Kazakhstan and also people, who disliked me with a passion; I never managed to get them to change their mind.

I have tried hard to get perceived by them differently but I learned that a first impression sticks and that focusing on getting it right was very important, as correcting it later could become extremely difficult.

Despite the fact that they disliked me and that, to be fair, the reciprocity was not completely false either, meeting them regularly and working alongside them has taught me a lot about perception and credibility.

Michael Bradley, former Ulster Bank Executive and former CEO of the Irish Franchising Association, whom I was lucky to have as mentor at the very start of my entrepreneurial journey.

I remember early morning meetings, going through my never ending first business plan and financial projections. I am very grateful to Michael for his constant support during a period of doubts, while trying to create a multi-million Euro business from scratch.

Edward Michael "Bear" Grylls, British adventurer, writer and television presenter, who was the youngest Briton to climb the Everest, and who travelled the world with his television series "Born Survivor" also known as "Man vs. Wild" in some countries.

Bear Grylls has been an inspiration for me in terms of perseverance and determination in the most difficult situations imaginable and by constantly overcoming challenges presented before him, with a smile. I watched him on TV for years and keep doing so with great pleasure even today.

I got a lot of energy and boost at the most needed times by watching him getting out of drastic situations. I drew a parallel with business and Start-Ups, for the survival mode you must enter into at times, in order to come on top of extreme situations, and the importance of knowledge.

Sean Bolger and **Brian O'Donohue**, Entrepreneurs and founders of Imagine Communications, a multi-million worth Telecom company built from scratch.

They took me under their wings for nearly a year and gave me a crash course in business.

I have seen the backstage of a successful business venture. They taught me an invaluable amount of things and helped me understand what really matters in business and what really doesn't.

Both Sean and Brian gave me a way of thinking outside the box and made business clearer for me. I will be always grateful to them for this.

www.potemkininc.com

Scan this QR code to visit
the www.potemkininc.com website
on your mobile phone.

www.ingramcontent.com/pod-product-compliance
Lightning Source LLC
Chambersburg PA
CBHW030008190526
45157CB00014B/1066